The Basics
of
Public Speaking

Edited by
Robert Trapp

with contributions by
Martin Remland
Robert Ross
Dennis Warnemunde

University of Northern Colorado

Kendall/Hunt
Publishing Company
Dubuque, Iowa

This edition has been printed directly from camera-ready copy.

Printed in the United States of America
10 9 8 7 6 5 4 3 2

Any department chair should be so lucky
to have such a great secretary

Without her help we would
not have been able to
write this book.

So,

We affectionately dedicate
this book to

Janet McDonald

TABLE OF CONTENTS

Chapter One

Introduction To Public Speaking

By

Robert Trapp

Speech contributes to our humanity in important ways. In terms
of evolution, the development of speech seems to have been parallel
to the development of the species homo sapien. Suzanne Langer
argues that the development of syntactic speech was a key factor in
the great leap from ape to human. In terms of the development of
human culture, few would deny the importance of the role of speech.
In fact some have maintained that the development of this uniquely
human form of communication was responsible for the development of
human culture (White). In our own culture the placement of freedom
of speech in the first amendment to the constitution was not
accidental.

Most of you are enrolled in your first course in speech and some
of you may be wondering why your graduation requirements include
such a course since you have been talking almost your entire life.
Since the power of speech seems to be the only thing that separates
humans from the rest of the animal kingdom, why do we require
students to take a course designed to develop skill in speech? This
seems almost like a course in advanced walking.

Still, while we have been speaking since our infancy, the mere
suggestion that we deliver a speech in public strikes terror into
the hearts of the brave. Although most of us are able to carry on a
conversation with a great deal of comfort, something about the
public speaking situation causes this sense of comfort to be
replaced with fear and uncertainty. So, while we may all consider

ourselves competent at conversational speaking, that mystical
something about P U B L I C   S P E A K I N G makes it a different
situation entirely.

CLASSICAL AND MODERN VIEWS OF PUBLIC SPEAKING

Public speaking today is different although no less important
than during the classical age of Greece and Rome. In both cultures
public speaking played an important role.

Public Speaking in Classical Times

Classical Greece was very much an oral society where the art of
public speaking was practiced in a variety of arenas. Three
conditions made that society ripe for the development of the art of
public speaking. First, the assembly was a major political
institution where any 20-year-old male could be a member. Second,
the Greek society included a popular jury system where the emphasis
for defense was on good speaking skills and finally, the whole Greek
society was an oral one; plays and literature were written to be
read aloud.

In classical times, the practice of public speaking was called
rhetoric and the effectiveness of a public speaker was judged by his
(yes, the practice of rhetoric generally was restricted to males)
skill in language and delivery. In fact, oratory was a contest in
the Olympic games and as such was judged entirely on the delivery of
the speaker. Perhaps this emphasis on style and delivery is the
reason that the term "rhetoric" has a negative meaning such as that
contained in the sentence "President Reagan's speech was full of
rhetoric and little else."

The orator was expected to conform to certain rules of delivery
that would seem very artificial in modern society. In the following
quotation the famous Greek teacher Quintilian described how an
orator should conduct himself regarding delivery:

> When called, he rises and secures a few moments for
> reflection while he arranges his toga. He then turns to
> the judge, but still does not launch into his speech. A
> dramatic tension is built up as he strokes his head, or
> looks at his hands, or even sighs. Then, feet slightly
> apart, standing straight but not stiffly, his face serious

but not sad, his arms slightly out from the body, his
right hand extending from the folds of his toga before his
breast, his thumb upward, fingers slightly bent, ready to
move out toward the right, he begins to speak, calmly,
with dignity.

Anyone speaking like this in modern society might well be committed
to a mental institution. Speech practices of today are certainly
less formal.

Public Speaking and Modern Society

One of the greatest speakers in the U.S. Senate was Senator
Everett M. Dirkson. Although some have said that oratory died with
his passing, we think that rumors of its death have been exaggerated
at least somewhat. While formal, stylistic oratory still exists in
some churches in this country, it has generally been replaced with a
conversational style of speech. The conversational style of Ronald
Reagan is a case in point. Called by many "the great communicator,"
Reagan might not have been considered a great orator. Still, he is
perceived by many to be a sincere, conversational speaker.

Public Speaking holds a vital role in many arenas in modern
society; arenas such as business, law, politics, and education. We
will briefly expand on two of these arenas.

Public Speaking and the World of Business

Public speaking is extremely important to today's business
person. Researchers have discovered that top managers in
Pennsylvania believed that the development of communication skills
was the most pressing educational need in their organization (Speech
Communication Association). One of the most needed skills involves
public speaking. In fact, for a mere $900, you can take a three day
course in public speaking from the American Management Association
covering topics such as introductory talks, impromptu speeches,
delivery, organization, audience analysis, answering questions, and
persuasion (Spectra).

The business person is frequently expected to prepare and
present informative reports or sales presentations. These reports
and presentations are expected to be well organized and presented in
a clear and interesting manner. Business executives have no
patience for a disorganized speaker whom they can't understand.

Public Speaking and the World of Education

While lecturing and giving a formal speech are different experiences, they have enough in common that improving one's public speaking skills will certainly improve one's lecturing skills. Of course lecturing is a very small part of what one does as a teacher. Teachers organize small groups, lead discussions, communicate interpersonally with students, and engage in a variety of activities other than public speaking. Why, then, should prospective teachers be concerned with improving their public speaking skills?

Teachers are important members of the society at large, and as such are often called on to present messages to groups of people other than their students. When they do this they need to be able to organize their ideas so that they are clear and understandable to the public at large. So, while teachers can improve themselves as teachers by nurturing their public speaking skills, more importantly, they can improve themselves as citizens and as people.

DEVELOPING PUBLIC SPEAKING SKILLS

While we will cover some of the theoretical aspects of public communication, we are interested primarily in skill development. Specifically, we will focus on the skills of speech composition, visual aids, handling audience questions, argumentation and persuasion, and delivery.

Our approach to developing public speaking skills is guided by three principles: First, we believe in certain minimal requirements for competence in public speaking; second, we believe that certain elementary principles must be mastered before one can be truly creative in the art of public speaking and third, we believe in the importance of constructive criticism.

The Minimal Requirements for Effective Public Speaking

In various chapters we will discuss each of these skills in depth. As we do, we will focus on what we call the "minimal requirements for competence." We believe that the development of competence in public speaking involves skill in each of the areas that we have mentioned.

By way of analogy, an English composition professor might say that the minimal requirements for competence in English composition involve grammar, mechanics, punctuation, spelling, diction, and effective sentences. A student who demonstrates skill in mechanics, punctuation, spelling, diction, effective sentences, but not in grammar has not met the minimal requirements of competence in English composition. And, having superior skill in spelling will not make up for failing to meet the minimal requirements in grammar.

At a more microscopic level, each of these skills can be further defined by the criteria necessary to accomplish them. So for instance, effective grammar must include sentence sense, avoidance of fragments and comma splices, proper use of adjectives and adverbs, agreement of subject and verb, etc. Thus, the student who meets all of those conditions, except agreement of subject and verb, cannot be said to have met the minimal conditions for grammar. And, once again, a student who is perfect at avoiding sentence fragments, but does not use proper subject and verb agreement cannot be said to have met the minimal conditions for effective grammar.

Similarly, in the public speaking situation, we have defined the skills that constitute the minimal requirements for competence in public speaking; speech composition, visual aids, handling audience questions, argumentation and persuasion, and delivery. In order to be competent in public speaking, one must meet certain necessary criteria in each of these areas. These criteria will be spelled out in more detail in later chapters. The important point to remember is that one must concentrate on developing skill in each of these areas and must concentrate on meeting all of the criteria within each area.

The Role of Creativity

At its finest, public speaking is a creative art. It is, however, an art that most of us develop one step at a time. First, we learn the basics of speech composition. Having only mastered the basics of speech composition, we may sound rather mechanical as we go through the motions of delivering signposts, internal summaries, and transitions. Having learned these basics we are then free to experiment--to develop our own individual style of practicing the art.

But, just as a swimmer learns the crawl before the butterfly and an artist paints still life before abstract art, the speaker also must master the basics before becoming a true artist. In this text we will focus on these basics. Lest we be misunderstood, we do not believe that one must follow these basics throughout life as if they were some ultimate laws. Our hope is that during this course you will master these basics and that you will then work to develop your own individual, creative style of public speaking.

The Role of Criticism and Evaluation

One important element of a person's public speaking ability involves nature--the natural talents that the person was born with and has developed further throughout life. Another is nurture--the development of our skills by practice and teaching. While we will not try to settle the age old debate about the relative importance of nature and nurture, we will argue that the latter is related to public speaking skill in important ways. In other words, even though we are all born with different talents, our skills in the area of public speaking can be improved with practice and teaching.

One of the most important aspects of a public speaking course is constructive criticism. Criticism succeeds only when both teacher and student are willing to invest the energy to make it work. The role of the instructor is to provide criticism that will allow you both to identify and correct your shortcomings. This is not an easy task. Most persons, teachers included, would rather compliment than criticize. Yet, the teacher who only compliments is providing a disservice to the student.

Your instructor will be devoting a great deal of energy and attention to your speech in order to give you oral and written comments that will help make you a better speaker. But, as we have said, constructive criticism is a two-sided coin. While the instructor must perform the task of evaluating and criticizing your speech, you must be willing to adopt a non-defensive posture in order to receive the criticism. If you adopt the kind of posture that says "My speech was perfect and anyone who says otherwise is a fool," you will receive minimal benefits from the criticism, your speeches may not improve, and harsh feelings will probably develop between you and your instructor. If, on the other hand, you are able to detach yourself so that you can listen to and read your instructor's comments with some sense of objectivity and detachment, your speeches will continue to improve. Some of us take criticism better than others. Some of us become down right defensive when someone points out that our work is less than perfect.

Chapter Two

Managing Stagefright

By

Martin Remland

Imagine yourself sitting in a public speaking class on the first
day of the new academic year. Your instructor, a very serious
looking gentleman, enters the classroom and immediately distributes
the course syllabus without uttering a single word. Casually
looking over the syllabus, you notice that a speech is scheduled for
the first day. You begin to get a little concerned and feel your
pulse quickening. You think to yourself, "he can't schedule a speech
on the first day of class." Suddenly, he loudly proclaims that the
first speech will begin today and that it will not only be graded on
both content and delivery but will represent a third of your final
grade in the course! Perspiration begins to appear on your brow.
According to his instructions, when your name is called you'll be
allowed to choose one of three possible topics and then will have 30
seconds to begin your presentation. As you wait and wonder whether
or not your name will be called, you experience the following
unpleasant sensations: your stomach feels empty and queasy, your
hands begin to shake, your mouth gets dry, you feel faint. Worst of
all, you can't remember your name or where you are. Slipping out
the back door, you resolve never to return.

Fortunately for most students who take a public speaking course,
such a nightmare is extremely unlikely. Recognizing the problem of
stage fright, which is alarmingly widespread, very few instructors
would dream of inflicting such additional pain on their students as
the fictional instructor described above does. The fact is that
most of us probably have experienced some degree of stage fright at
one time or another. And, surprisingly, more people are afraid of
public speaking than you might realize. Asking some 3000 people
what their greatest fears were, a group of researchers discovered
that more people were afraid of speaking before a group (40.6%) than

were afraid of financial problems (22%), loneliness (13.6%), deep water (21.5%) sickness (18.8%), heights (32%), and even death (18.7%). For some reason, nothing scared the respondents in the survey more than the prospect of public speaking (R. H. Bruskin Associates, 1973).

In this chapter, we will explore the problem of stage fright. In the first section, I discuss the meaning of stage fright as it relates to public speaking. In the next two sections, I explain the basic causes of stage fright and the symptoms most commonly associated with it. Finally, and most importantly, I describe a number of techniques that can reduce the fear of giving a speech. Although I generally will use the term stage fright in my discussion, I should point out that other terms such as speech anxiety, and speaking apprehension are synonymous with stage fright and are used quite often by writers on this subject.

THE MEANING OF STAGE FRIGHT

To begin with, I should tell you what I mean by stage fright. Stage fright refers to the mental and physical manifestations of the fear associated with a public performance. Whenever we do something that is observed and judged by others, we are, in effect, giving a performance. Certainly, the performance doesn't need to be on a stage for us to be judged by others. Everyday, people get stage fright waiting to be interviewed for a job, being introduced to an important person or group, or going out on a date. The most significant factor is that we are (or think we are) being evaluated in a critical manner.

The fear we experience in such situations leads to an array of physical and mental reactions referred to as the "symptoms" of stage fright. These symptoms can range from a little nervous energy, which might indicate a very mild case of stage fright, to various sensations that can make us feel nauseous, panicky, forgetful, and faint. But the manifestations of stage fright include the thoughts we have in addition to our physiological responses. The desire to escape, the feeling of insecurity, and the belief that we are being laughed at by our audience, all represent the mental symptoms of stage fright.

Even though many of the symptoms I've listed above are quite unpleasant, I don't want to give you the impression that stage fright is necessarily a problem for public speakers. It can be when the symptoms become so overwhelming that we are unable to speak effectively or when the symptoms are so severe that we become sick or depressed before, during, or after the presentation. When these

things happen we consider stage fright debilitating. But stage
fright also can be facilitating to a speaker. A mild case of stage
fright gives us the extra energy we need to be alert and expressive
on our feet. I've had more than a few days when, due to a lack of
energy, I felt more like taking a nap than talking to a class. And
I usually get a little nervous on days like that because I fear not
being able to recall what I want to say. But as soon as I get in
front of a class I notice a dramatic difference in the way I feel,
especially when I begin speaking. Suddenly I feel a surge of energy
and the words seem to come from nowhere. I feel sharper and more
enthusiastic than I felt just minutes earlier. To most public
speakers, this is a very common experience and a direct result of
the nervous energy associated with stage fright.

So, stage fright can be facilitating or debilitating in its
effect on a speaker. But, some people are more likely than others
to experience the debilitating effects of stage fright. Using the
term "public speaking apprehension," rather than stage fright, Dr.
James McCroskey, Professor of Speech Communication at West Virginia
University, devised a test to measure the likelihood that an
individual will experience the debilitating effects of public
speaking anxiety. The test consists of 34 statements. You indicate
how much you agree or disagree with each statement by circling the
appropriate response. For each statement, you note whether you:
strongly agree (SA), agree (A), are undecided (U), disagree (D), or
strongly disagree (SD). Since you'll be giving several speeches in
this course, I recommend taking the test to assess your own level of
stage fright or anxiety at this point in time. Perhaps after you
complete the course, you should take the test again to see if you
have become a more confident public speaker. Go ahead and take the
test now. Work quickly and record your first impressions. After
you finish the test I'll explain how you determine your score.

		SA	A	U	D	SD
1.	While preparing for a speech, I feel tense and nervous.	5	4	3	2	1
2.	I feel tense when I see the words "speech" and "public speech" on a course outline when studying.	5	4	3	2	1
3.	My thoughts become confused and jumbled when I am giving a speech.	5	4	3	2	1
4.	Right after giving a speech, I feel that I have had a pleasant experience.	1	2	3	4	5
5.	I get anxious when I think about a speech coming up.	5	4	3	2	1
6.	I have no fear of giving a speech.	1	2	3	4	5
7.	Although I am nervous just before starting a speech, I soon settle down after starting and feel calm and comfortable.	1	2	3	4	5
8.	I look forward to giving a speech.	1	2	3	4	5
9.	When the instructor announces a speaking assignment in class, I can feel myself getting tense.	5	4	3	2	1
10.	My hands tremble when I am giving a speech.	5	4	3	2	1
11.	I feel relaxed while giving a speech.	1	2	3	4	5
12.	I enjoy preparing for a speech.	1	2	3	4	5
13.	I am in constant fear of forgetting what I am prepared to say.	5	4	3	2	1
14.	I get anxious if someone asks me something about my topic that I do not know.	5	4	3	2	1
15.	I face the prospect of giving a speech with confidence.	1	2	3	4	5
16.	I feel that I am in complete possession of myself while giving a speech.	1	2	3	4	5
17.	My mind is clear when giving a speech.	1	2	3	4	5
18.	I do not dread giving a speech.	1	2	3	4	5
19.	I perspire just before starting a speech.	5	4	3	2	1
20.	My heart beats very fast just as I start a speech.	5	4	3	2	1
21.	I experience considerable anxiety while sitting in the room just before my speech starts.	5	4	3	2	1

		SA	A	U	D	SD
22.	Certain parts of my body feel very tense and rigid while giving a speech.	5	4	3	2	1
23.	Realizing that only a little time remains in a speech makes me very tense and anxious.	5	4	3	2	1
24.	While giving a speech, I know I can control my feelings of tension and stress.	1	2	3	4	5
25.	I breathe faster just before starting a speech.	5	4	3	2	1
26.	I feel comfortable and relaxed in the hour or so just before giving a speech.	1	2	3	4	5
27.	I do poorly in speeches because I am anxious.	5	4	3	2	1
28.	I feel anxious when the teacher announces the date of a speaking assignment.	5	4	3	2	1
29.	When I make a mistake while giving a speech, I find it hard to concentrate on the parts that follow.	5	4	3	2	1
30.	During an important speech, I experience a feeling of helplessness building up inside me.	5	4	3	2	1
31.	I have trouble falling asleep the night before a speech.	5	4	3	2	1
32.	My heart beats very fast while I present a speech.	5	4	3	2	1
33.	I feel anxious while waiting to give my speech.	5	4	3	2	1
34.	While giving a speech, I get so nervous I forget facts I really know.	5	4	3	2	1

To compute your score on the test, simply total the numbers you circled. Scores on this test can range from a low of 34 to a high of 170. The average (mean) score for college undergraduates is about 115. Approximately 68% of the students who complete this test are likely to score between 98 and 132. If you scored above 132, you are among about 16% of the college population who report a high degree of stage fright. A score below 98 puts you in the 16% of students with very little fear of public speaking.

Of course, a major limitation of this test is that it doesn't take into account the many circumstances surrounding a particular speech that either can increase or decrease the degree of anxiety we experience. For example, you probably will feel a lot more relaxed giving a speech to a small audience of friends than to a large audience of strangers. Similarly, wouldn't you feel more nervous talking about a topic you don't understand than about a topic you understand very well? These factors bring up an important distinction that needs to be made between the "trait" versus the "state" nature of stage fright. Stage fright is considered a public speaking trait when the person in question is afraid of giving speeches regardless of the situation. Your score on the test you just took is a measure of stage fright as a trait. It determined your general tendency to be fearful of giving a speech. When viewed as a state, however, the amount of stage fright we experience depends on the particular situation. For me, personally, it depends almost entirely on how prepared I am. When I feel ready to go, there's no problem. But I'm a nervous wreck when I don't or can't prepare as fully as I'd like to.

THE CAUSES OF STAGE FRIGHT

Why are so many people afraid of giving speeches? The idea that some people are more afraid of giving a speech than they are of dying may seem utterly absurd. But there is little doubt that being called on to speak in public can be a hair-raising experience. In this section I'll discuss some of the reasons why.

Recall earlier that I defined stage fright, essentially, as the fear of a public performance. In the special case of public speaking it represents the fear of speaking to a group of people. But since speaking is such a natural activity why should this be so frightening? The primary reason is that we are afraid of a potentially disapproving audience. Our self-concept, wrapped up as it is in the impressions of those around us, is quite vulnerable to the judgments of others. And when those judgments are unfavorable, most of us will tend to think less of ourselves as a result. Few people are unaffected by negative feedback, no matter what they might say or who they happen to be. Since, in a public speaking situation, an extraordinary amount of attention is focused on the speaker, the chance of being "put down" is much greater than it is in ordinary social encounters.

Of course, it doesn't matter whether or not the fear is justified but only that it exists. In fact, most of the disturbing thoughts we have about our performance and about the reactions of our audience are greatly exaggerated, as I will show in my section on managing stage fright. Some of the things speakers fear include: looking unattractive, boring their audience, saying something stupid, doing something inappropriate, being seen as incompetent,

and feeling physically ill. Added to all of this is the fear of the
unknown--not knowing exactly what to expect. While this is only a
partial list of the fears that are possible, it does give us a
pretty good picture of the damage to our egos we might envision
taking place if we're forced to give a speech.

     The fear we are likely to experience is very situational; many
different things can increase or decrease the fear. I'll briefly
mention what I consider to be the seven most significant factors.

1.   THE SIZE OF THE AUDIENCE--Generally people tend to be more
     afraid of speaking to a large rather than to a small group of
     people. This makes a lot of sense since stage fright is a
     product of what is thought to be audience disapproval. The
     larger the audience, the greater the potential for rejection.
     It's one thing to make a fool of yourself in front of 10
     people; it's another thing entirely to do it in front of 100.
     But this apparent effect isn't true for everyone. Some people,
     in many cases experienced performers, find the increased
     intimacy of a small gathering much more intimidating than a
     large audience.

2.   THE STATUS OF THE AUDIENCE--Not all audience disapproval is
     valued equally by a speaker. The "weight" given to the
     disapproval of a particular audience depends on how powerful
     the audience is, as determined by their ability to reward or
     punish the speaker. For this reason, you might become more
     nervous giving a presentation to the professors in your
     department than to a group of your peers, assuming the former
     are more powerful than the latter in your opinion.

3.   THE CLOSENESS OF THE AUDIENCE--Would you be more nervous
     speaking to a group of strangers or to a group of close
     friends? Chances are if you could choose your audience you'd
     prefer to talk to your friends. Part of the explanation is the
     increased uncertainty we experience when interacting with
     strangers. Our natural fear of the unknown leads to a
     condition often referred to as "stranger anxiety." And, rather
     than put up with the discomfort of meeting new people, many
     choose to avoid interpersonal contacts as much as possible.
     This fear of the unknown, in the form of stranger anxiety,
     leads many people to become shy and withdrawn. In addition,
     there is a natural inclination to think that strangers will be
     more disapproving than our friends will be. After all, our
     friends already have seen us do and say dumb things and they're

still our friends. Thus, being rejected by our friends is a
lot less risky than being rejected by strangers.

4.   PRIOR EXPERIENCES--Have you ever given a speech before?
      Perhaps you've given an oral report in a class. If the
      experience was a bad one because of your nervousness (i.e. you
      couldn't stop perspiring, you had trouble breathing), because
      of how you affected your audience (i.e. some couldn't stop
      smirking while others fell asleep), or because of how the
      instructor reacted (i.e. he or she gave you an F- and insulted
      you mercilessly), it would be awfully difficult to get
      enthusiastic about giving another presentation. In
      behavioristic terms, we would say that you have been
      "negatively reinforced" to avoid speaking in public. That
      means avoidance behavior, ranging from writing papers instead
      of doing oral reports to choosing careers that don't involve
      any chance of public speaking, has been rewarded. And it's
      likely that avoidance behavior will continue until you
      experience the positive outcomes of giving a speech (i.e.
      expressing yourself, influencing others, feeling invigorated,
      meeting new people, making a good impression, etc.) which can
      be very satisfying.

5.   FOCUSING ON THE FEAR--Have you ever tried not to think about
      something someone tells you not to think about? For example,
      you're told: "for the next 30 seconds do not think about
      chocolate ice cream." You'll probably have a lot of trouble
      trying to get the image of chocolate ice cream out of your
      mind. How much easier it would be not to think about chocolate
      ice cream if our instructions were to concentrate for the next
      30 seconds on the beauty of a full moon. Similarly, the very
      act of trying not to think about how nervous we are just before
      giving a speech or while we are giving it is likely to make us
      more nervous. We'll have trouble getting the symptoms of stage
      fright (i.e. sweaty palms, dry mouth, shaking knees, etc.) out
      of our mind. In essence, a "vicious cycle" is created where
      recognizing the signs of stage fright makes us more fearful
      which in turn makes the signs of stage fright more noticeable
      to us.

      I had an unpleasant experience not too long ago when, in the
      middle of lecturing on a topic I didn't know a great deal about
      (which was sufficient cause for some anxiety on my part), I
      suddenly became aware of my nervousness. At that point, I
      began to hesitate slightly. I then felt that my hesitations
      were picked up by the class which caused me to lose some

confidence in my presentation. That lost confidence then showed up in my inability to concentrate on what I was saying. Luckily, I was able to call a break since this happened at the end of a one-hour session. And, I'm happy to report that I was able to regain my composure for the second hour.

6. BELIEFS ABOUT PUBLIC SPEAKING--Not surprisingly, inexperienced speakers have a number of misconceptions about public speaking that cause them to feel more fearful than they should. I'd like to address what I consider to be the three most destructive beliefs.

The first is the belief that we are transparent. What I mean by this is that, contrary to all of the available data, many beginning speakers think that their audience not only can see how fast their heart is beating but can easily discern their every intention (i.e. "they know I'm exaggerating", "they can see I'm pretending to be enthusiastic", etc.). In truth, scientific research shows that listeners usually are unable to determine whether or not a speaker is nervous or whether or not a speaker is being deceptive.

A second belief that increases speech anxiety is that we will be less fearful if we minimize our contact with the audience. This false belief leads to advice that you should try not to look at your audience (i.e. read your speech, look at the back wall in the room, look at their foreheads, etc.). In fact, the opposite is true. Avoidance behavior, such as not looking at people in the audience, will increase stage fright. There are many reasons for this. One concerns the negative reactions of an audience to a speaker's lack of eye contact. These negative reactions, interpreted by the speaker as evidence of disapproval, will invariably lead to a loss of confidence and hence more nervousness. I'll explain later how increased eye contact decreases stage fright.

The third belief that causes increased anxiety is that we will give a better speech if we choose our words in advance. On the face of it, this sounds pretty convincing. While I don't dispute the need to prepare a speech, unless the speaking occasion is extremely formal (i.e. the speech will be transcribed for posterity or it will be quoted extensively by the media), trying to stick to a "script" is very unwise. First, if you try to memorize words rather than ideas, there's a good chance you won't remember some of the words. And forgetting will make you more nervous. But even if you remember the exact words, without practice or training in expressive speech, you're likely to "sound" as though you're reading rather than talking. If your weak delivery turns off the audience, their reactions will increase your anxiety. Second, if you stick to your script by reading most of your speech, you'll be avoiding the audience and that will increase your anxiety as well.

7.   PREPARATION--Of all the variables that affect stage fright, I regard preparation as the most important. But the factor I'm focusing on here isn't whether a speaker prepares or not; it's the way a speaker prepares. As I mentioned above, preparing for a classroom speech by writing out the entire speech probably will increase rather than decrease stage fright. In contrast, a systematic approach to speech preparation, such as the one I'll briefly outline in the final section of this chapter, is likely to decrease speech anxiety. If we prepare properly for a speech we'll feel more confident than we would feel without such preparation. In addition, the reactions of the audience will be more favorable than they would be otherwise.

To briefly review, stage fright is caused by a speaker's fear of a disapproving audience. That fear probably will increase when the audience is either larger or smaller than the speaker desires, when the audience can exercise power over the speaker, when the audience consists of strangers rather than friends, when a speaker has had previous public speaking experiences that were unpleasant, when a speaker pays too much attention to his/her signs of nervousness, when a speaker holds misconceptions about giving speeches, and when a speaker doesn't properly prepare to speak.

THE SYMPTOMS OF STAGE FRIGHT

The fear of performing in public results in various physical and psychological reactions. These reactions are the symptoms of stage fright; the manifestations of our fear. In this section I'll describe three basic types: fight or flight reactions, avoidance displays, and fear-related thoughts.

Fight or Flight Reactions

Nature has endowed us with the capacity to respond quickly and unconsciously to dangerous situations. When faced with danger, real or imagined, a number of physiological changes take place within our bodies that are designed to mobilize us for fighting or fleeing in response to the danger. These bodily reactions provide us with the energy we need in emergency situations. Some of the most common symptoms are described briefly below:

1. Accelerated Heart Rate--this occurs because more blood is pumped to the skeletal muscles in preparation for a physical response.

2. Rapid Breathing--we might experience some difficulty breathing as the body increases its supply of oxygen in anticipation of exertion.

3. Blanching--we become pale when the peripheral blood vessels, near the surface of the body, are contracted in order to increase the blood pressure needed for an emergency.

4. Perspiration--the body breaks out in a "cold sweat" in preparation for the warm sweat associated with physical activity.

5. Queasy Stomach--we get "butterflies" when blood leaves the muscles of the stomach and intestines for the skeletal muscles.

6. Empty Stomach--digestive activity is suspended in anticipation of physical exertion; gastric juices in the stomach decrease.

7. Dry Mouth--this sensation occurs because of the decrease in saliva associated with the relative inactivity of the digestive system.

8. Wide Eyes--as part of our natural facial expression of fear, it is theorized that our eyes widen in order to facilitate greater vision of impending danger.

The physiological responses listed above are adapted from the "classic" study by Rollo May, one of the leading authorities on the nature of anxiety. While there are many other physiological responses associated with fear and anxiety, the ones listed above, seem to be a representative sample. Dr. May stresses the importance of these symptoms as follows:

> Originally in the time of primitive man, these responses had a clear purpose in protecting the person from wild animals and other concrete perils. In modern society man

has few direct threats; the anxiety mainly concerns such
psychological states as social alienation, competitive
success, and so on. But the mechanisms for coping with
threats remain the same (May, 1977, p. 69).

Avoidance Displays

Another class of stage fright symptoms express a speaker's
desire to avoid the situation he or she is in. These behaviors
suggest that the speaker is feeling insecure and would like to be
somewhere else. They can include:

- lack of eye contact with the audience
- standing far away from the audience
- lack of movement toward the audience
- rapid rate of speech
- omitting parts of the speech
- standing behind a lectern
- folding arms
- touching self

Perhaps the most common avoidance display is not looking at the
audience. This can take many forms. Some speakers rarely look at
the audience, preferring instead to read their speeches. Some nod
their heads up and down at a fairly rapid rate, glancing at the
audience or their notes for one or two seconds at a time. Some
feign eye contact with their audience and fix their gaze instead on
something in the room such as the back wall.

Avoidance also is rather apparent in a speaker's attempt to end
the presentation as quickly as possible, such as talking very fast
or deliberately leaving things out of the speech. And, actions that
"shield" the speaker from the audience, regardless of whether they
are intentional (i.e. standing behind and clutching the lectern) or
not (i.e. folding arms across chest or touching face), signal the
speaker's desire to avoid the situation. In particular, research
studies in the field of nonverbal communication have found that
various acts of self-touching, often referred to as "adaptors", tend
to increase in stressful situations (Matarazzo, Harper, and Wiens,
1978).

Fear-Related Thoughts

The anxiety associated with public speaking gives rise to all sorts of thoughts that reflect and reinforce the stage fright of a speaker. These thoughts express the negative feelings the speaker is having toward the entire public speaking episode. They are symptomatic of the speaker's fear of audience rejection. Some commonly reported thoughts that occur prior to speaking are:

"They are going to be bored with my presentation."
"I'll never be able to remember what I want to say."
"What are they going to think about my appearance?"
"I don't want to give this speech."

More serious, perhaps, are the feelings we have while speaking. When a speaker becomes self-conscious during his or her presentation, attention is focused away from the ideas that need to be communicated to the speech anxiety itself. Here are some typical thoughts:

"My voice sounds like it's quivering."
"I don't know what to do with my hands."
"I hope my hair looks OK".
"They can tell I'm nervous."
"I can't wait until this is over."
"Am I sweating?"
"Oh no, my hands are shaking."
"How come he's staring at me like I'm an idiot?"

What do all of these thoughts have in common? First they are the result of a speaker's fear of audience disapproval; second they make a speaker feel very self-conscious; and third they focus a speaker's attention on how fearful he or she is.

As we can see, there are more than a few symptoms of stage fright. If you experience fear before or during your speech, you may become cognizant of various fight or flight reactions, avoidance displays, and fear-related thoughts. Hopefully, these symptoms will not have a debilitating effect because you will be able to manage them successfully.

MANAGING STAGE FRIGHT

Before I begin listing the myriad of coping techniques available to a frightened speaker, let me emphasize a few preliminary points. First, every public speaker should realize that some degree of stage fright is beneficial. As I noted earlier, many of the symptoms of stage fright are nothing more than the body's natural reaction to a potential threat. These fight or flight responses prepare us to confront this threat by giving us a boost of extra energy. If we put this "nervous energy" to good use we'll give a much better speech than we would give if we were extremely relaxed.

Second, every public speaker should accept the fact that most of the symptoms will not be detected by the audience. Fortunately, those reactions that we have the least amount of control over, such as our pounding heart and shaking knees, also are the most difficult for the audience to see.

Finally, giving a speech usually turns out to be a lot easier than the novice thinks it's going to be. The experience reminds me of how I feel jumping into a cold swimming pool. Knowing it's cold always makes me apprehensive about jumping in, but once I do, it becomes an invigorating experience. Similarly, once you start talking I'll bet you won't know what you were afraid of. Now, for some concrete suggestions. Surprisingly, there is quite a bit of agreement among public speaking experts on what works and what doesn't. My list will consist of those techniques that I think are most effective and most practical at a certain point in time. First, I'll discuss the coping strategies that are appropriate several days before you are assigned to speak (these will be called phase I techniques). Then, I'll describe some methods that can be used to minimize anxiety while you're waiting in class for your turn to speak (referred to as phase II techniques). Finally, I'll identify the things that are most helpful during your speech (phase III techniques).

Techniques for Managing Stage Fright During Phase I

There is little mystery about what works best to minimize stage fright during phase I. The three things are: preparing properly, practicing, and adopting a positive outlook. The last recommendation probably will follow naturally from the first two because of the confidence you will have in your ability to give a good speech.

Prepare Properly for the Speech

The best way to guarantee that stage fright will be facilitating rather than debilitating is to prepare properly for your speech. It's hard to be scared to death when you know you're doing exactly what you're supposed to be doing. And as you follow the basic steps you'll be looking forward to the speech.

The first step is to pick a good topic. Your topic ought to be something you are very familiar with or are very interested in. This advice is especially important for beginning speakers. If you know a lot about your topic the whole idea of talking about it should seem less intimidating. If you care a great deal about your topic you'll be motivated to learn more about it and to tell others what you've discovered.

The second step is to narrow the topic to something manageable by deciding on a very specific purpose. What is it you want your audience to know, feel, believe, or do, after your speech? You ought to be able to express your purpose in a concise sentence.

The third step is to research your topic and think about it whenever you can. This means reading, taking notes, and talking about your ideas to friends. Your aim here should be, not only to learn more about your topic, but to collect information that will support and elucidate your ideas. Try to find material that will catch and keep our attention, such as startling facts, humorous anecdotes, vivid stories, thought provoking quotations, etc. And, use visual aids. Charts, graphs, pictures, props, etc. serve two important functions: they will make your presentation more interesting and they will divert some attention away from you while you are speaking so that you'll feel less self-conscious.

The fourth step is to outline your ideas. In the beginning, your outline should be as detailed as possible since your goal is to express your main points as logically and completely as you can, given the research you've done. But you'll need to adapt your outline to the speaking situation. This means cutting some things out of your original outline so you don't exceed the time limit set for the speech. It also means using "key words" rather than complete sentences to represent the points that were in your original outline. This technique is especially important. The key word outline is what you should use while giving your speech; the key words should serve to "trigger" your memory so you can talk about an idea without reading. By doing this, you'll be free to look at your audience (which actually reduces stage fright) and to focus your attention on the ideas you want to get across (which also reduces stage fright).

Practice Delivering the Speech

You should plan to finish preparing your speech a couple of days before you are scheduled to give it. This will give you some time to practice. Practice will take most of the uncertainty out of the public speaking experience. Surely you'll be more confident if you have a good idea of what you're going to do and say in advance. Even the most experienced entertainers, athletes, and speakers practice before they perform. I'll talk more about how to practice in the chapter on delivery.

Adopt a Positive Outlook

A positive outlook means that you are looking forward to giving your speech because you feel that you have something worthwhile to communicate. It means that you recognize how silly it is to dwell on all of the little things that make you self-conscious and that the audience will not notice anyway. It means that you find nothing horrible about being in a situation that naturally increases your adrenalin and your blood pressure. It means that you realize how unusually supportive your audience will be, since, being in the "same boat" they readily identify with you. It also means that you know, even if you feel the butterflies in your stomach as you walk to the front of the class, that they will be gone as soon as you start to speak. And finally, it means that you accept the principle that public speaking does, in fact, build self-confidence. The more you do it, the better you'll feel about yourself.

Techniques for Managing Stage Fright During Phase II

If you're like most people who have given speeches, you'll find the few minutes right before you're called on to give your speech to be the worst part of the whole experience. If you're going to get stage fright, that's when you're going to feel it the most. Of course, unless the symptoms are debilitating (i.e. you feel too sick to talk), they might not be worth worrying about. After all, a little nervous energy will help prepare you to be alert and expressive. Nevertheless, I want to suggest a few techniques that should prove helpful.

Take a Few Slow, Deep Breaths

The physiological symptoms of stage fright include rapid breathing and muscular tension. A few deep breaths, when held for a few seconds have been found to help relax the mind and the body. This is especially helpful a few minutes before speaking since that's when we're likely to be most anxious.

Engage in Constructive Self-Talk or Imagery

It's helpful to remind yourself of some of the things that characterize the positive outlook you have developed. For instance, you should become eager rather than apprehensive when you begin to think about telling your audience things they might know little or nothing about, or things that will amuse or startle them. You might try saying to yourself: "I have something very interesting to tell this class." Constructive imagery also can help. Try picturing some of the positive reactions you might get from the audience. Try imagining how fluent your speech will be, how expressive your voice will sound, or how effectively you'll present your visual aids.

Take Your Mind Off the Speech

For some, it's better not to think about the speech at all. A lot of beginning speakers have trouble focusing attention on positive self-talk or imagery and instead end up dwelling on all sorts of dreadful consequences or on their own nervous symptoms. Therefore, an alternative technique is to think about something else that is very likely to command your attention. If possible, try paying attention to what one of the other speakers is saying. After all, that is the courteous thing to do. And it will keep your mind off your speech. But, if that doesn't work and you're still very nervous, think about something else (i.e. try finding a solution to some difficult problem). Remember that fear-related thoughts are one of the major symptoms and instigators of stage fright.

Evoke a Different Emotion

This is another technique that tries to get you to focus your attention on something other than your stage fright. The basic principle is that it is difficult to fully feel more than one emotion at a time. If you are angry or happy, for example, you're not likely to feel much fear. Therefore, you might try getting yourself to focus on something (i.e. a recent experience) that will make you feel happy, angry, disgusted, sad, interested, etc. As I noted above, however, it is always preferable to pay attention to the other speakers in your class. If their speeches are interesting you won't have much to worry about.

Techniques for Managing Stage Fright During Phase III

Now you might be saying to yourself: "By the time I get up in front of the class it's too late. Nothing will help me now. I'm doomed to spend the next few minutes in agony." Surprisingly, there are a number of very effective techniques that can be used to reduce stage fright during this phase. The most important thing to remember, however, is the fact that most of your anxiety will disappear naturally once you start talking. Chances are good that your mind will be too busy trying to verbalize your ideas to focus on your emotional condition. But, just in case, here's what I recommend:

Get Off to a Good Start

To begin with, pause for a few seconds before you start to speak. These few seconds will give you some time to think through what you're going to say when you start talking, to make sure you have everything you need (i.e. notes, audio-visual aids, etc.), and to see if the audience is ready to listen. Don't start off with a comment about how nervous you are. That will make your audience uncomfortable and probably will trigger fear-related thoughts that will make you more nervous than you already are. Similarly, although I suggest taking a few deep breaths to help you relax while you're waiting your turn to speak, heavy breathing won't make a very good impression when you're standing in front of the class.

Use Notes to Facilitate Your Memory

A useful "rule-of-thumb" is to look at your notes about 10-20 percent of the time during your speech. Your speaking outline should be designed to jog your memory, not to replace it. When you look at the key words that represent a particular point in your outline, you should be able to start talking about that idea immediately, without reading and without trying to recall the exact words on some script. There's a big difference between remembering an idea and remembering the exact wording of that idea. Now, what effect does this use of notes have on stage fright? First, being able to look at your audience instead of your notes will minimize the avoidance behavior that is symptomatic of stage fright. Second, you'll find that it's much easier to remember one idea than it is remembering twenty-five words. And, if you've practiced expressing that idea the words will come quite readily, though they may change slightly from time to time.

Use Audio-Visual Aids

I consider this an excellent way to reduce stage fright. Aside from making your speech more interesting, which will result in positive feedback from the audience that will make you feel more confident, audio-visual aids allow you to shift the attention of the audience away from you personally. As a result, you naturally feel less self-conscious.

Move Occasionally

A lot of speakers freeze as soon as they get up in front of an audience to speak. This lack of movement increases stage fright for a couple of reasons. First, if the speaker doesn't move at all he or she will seem very unnatural to the audience; they probably will infer that the speaker is nervous. And their reactions will make the speaker feel even more nervous. Second, most speakers recognize their inability to move as a symptom of stage fright. That recognition, like the recognition of any sign of nervousness, can set off a vicious cycle of fear.

Some speakers, however, have the opposite problem--they move too much. Excessive movement, especially when it serves no discernable purpose, is also a symptom of stage fright. Movement should be purposeful. In the chapter on delivery, I'll discuss how movement can enhance the delivery of a speaker. For now, it's important merely to acknowledge the fact that some bodily movement can help a speaker release some of the nervous energy that is symptomatic of stage fright.

Behave in a Confident Manner

There's a substantial body of theory and research in the field of human emotions in support of the idea that we feel the way we act. While it is certainly an oversimplification to say that we'll feel better if we just "put on a happy face," there is reason to consider such advice more seriously than you might imagine. Discussing the intricate relationship between physical expression and human feelings, one of the leading authorities on the subject, Dr. Carroll E. Izard of Vanderbilt University, argues that, under certain circumstances, a behavioral display alone can change a person's emotional state.

> . . . the open and deliberate use of a specific voluntary expression to activate the corresponding subjective experience may be effective if the individual wants the experience (e.g. to bolster courage) and if inhibitory processes are not too strong. There are both neurological and psychological grounds for such emotion activation (Izard, 1977, p. 62.).

Apparently, there is some scientific basis for the belief that "whistling in the dark," can, to some extent, allay one's fear of walking around at night.

Put in perspective, there is good reason to believe that a public speaker can do certain things that will make him or her appear, and subsequently feel self-assured rather than frightened. These behaviors include: eye contact, gestures, good posture, and vocal projection. For specific guidelines on how to speak in a confident manner, please see the chapter on delivery.

Establish Eye Contact with Supportive Listeners

Let's face it. Some people are just poor listeners. They don't have much of an attention span and they're not courteous enough to put any effort into their listening. As you look out at your audience, you'll see friendly expressions, blank expressions, bored expressions, confused expressions, etc. Whenever you feel the need to get a little boost of confidence, look at the friendly, attentive faces in your audience and avoid looking at the others until you feel confident again. The general principle is to seek positive reinforcement when necessary. Looking at a friendly and attentive face will make you feel good. It's always nice to know that someone is interested in what you're saying.

SUMMARY

Stage fright refers to the mental and physical manifestations of the fear associated with a public performance. The fear of audience disapproval experienced by a speaker need not be debilitating. Rather, the nervous energy that results from a mild case of the "jitters" can facilitate the speaker's performance. The various symptoms of stage fright, which include fight or flight reactions, avoidance displays, and fear-related thoughts, are affected by a number of important factors. These factors are: the size of the speaker's audience, the status of the audience, how familiar the speaker is with the audience, the speaker's prior experiences in public speaking situations, how much the speaker focuses on his or her symptoms, the speaker's beliefs about public speaking, and how prepared the speaker is.

There are a number of things a speaker can do to cope with stage fright. Prior to the scheduled speech (phase I) proper preparation, practice, and a positive outlook will minimize a speaker's anxiety. During the second phase, which is while the speaker is waiting his/her turn to speak, the speaker might try to take a few deep breaths engage in constructive self-talk or imagery, avoid thinking about the speech, or evoke a different emotion. Finally, during the speech (phase III) a speaker is less likely to be nervous if he or she gets off to a good start, uses notes effectively, uses audio-visual aids, moves to release excess energy, behaves in a confident manner, and establishes eye contact with supportive listeners.

Chapter Three

Speech Composition

By

Dennis Warnemunde

Human beings have an innate desire to organize. They strive
for unity and harmony--order rather than chaos. Kenneth E. Boulding
(1956) explains this tendency to strive for organization when he
states that:

> It is the capacity for organizing information into large
> and complex images which is the chief glory of our
> species. . . . Our image of time. . .goes far beyond that
> of most intelligence of lower animals, mainly because of
> our capacity for language and for record. . . . Closely
> associated with the time structure of his [human being's]
> image is the image of the structure of relationships.
> Because we are aware of time, we are also aware of cause
> and effect, of contiguity and succession of cycles and
> repetition (p. 25).

The organization of a speech is one application of this human
talent for organizing our environment into thoughts and ideas that
we want to convey to others. This process of organizing a speech is
not an easy task. However, since we share "the structure of
relationships," it is possible to communicate with some accuracy our
basic thoughts and experiences to others. "Even listeners with poor
perceptions can see relationships if we organize our thoughts with
careful regard for the patterns all men [persons] are accustomed to
perceiving" (Wilson & Arnold, 1974, p. 165).

The techniques for organizing an informative or persuasive speech are very similar. In the context of planning and organizing materials, two processes, analysis and synthesis, are involved. Analysis is "the process of investigating a subject or problem to see what it involves, resolving it into its constituents, and discovering how the parts relate to the whole and the whole to its parts" (Bryant & Wallace, 1969, p. 131). This process of analysis begins when you have a vague notion of a speech topic and you review your background and experiences to determine what the subject involves. It continues more formally as you collect information about the subject (i.e., talking to others about the topic, researching the topic in the library, interviewing authorities on the topic).

Synthesis is "putting the material of a speech together for the purpose one has in mind" (Bryant & Wallace, p. 132). In developing a speech, synthesis involves three main steps: (1) determining the speech purpose, (2) selecting relevant materials for the speech, and (3) organizing the relevant ideas so that members of the audience can "perceive them clearly and remember them easily" (Bryant & Wallace, p. 132).

This chapter will consider selecting the speech topic; formulating the speech purpose and thesis statement; preparing the introduction, body, and conclusion of the speech; using transitions, signposts, and internal summaries; and designing the speech outline.

SELECTING THE SPEECH TOPIC

In everyday life speakers customarily draw their topics from the speech occasion or from their areas of expertise: their social or political interest, their hobbies, or their profession or occupation. Unfortunately, because of inexperience and because of the artificial nature of the classroom environment, the selection of an appropriate speech subject can be a harrowing task for the beginning speaker.

The first step in selecting an appropriate speech subject is to examine your personal experiences to discover potential subjects that will meet the expectations of the audience and the speaking occasion. Do not blindfold yourself by thinking that nothing that you know would be of interest to anyone else. Before turning to external sources of information, focus on your present and past experiences or environment, your beliefs, attitudes, feelings, and desires. Try to dispel the typical false or negative defenses, such as "I'm not well informed on any subject," or "I'm not really interested in anything." If these statements were true, you would have lived the life of a vegetable, not the life of a thoughtful person in an ever-changing world.

Use the following list to examine your background and experiences. Try to identify two or three subjects that could be potential speech topics for each subcategory.

1.   "Life" Experiences

    a.   a medical condition you have
    b.   an unusual experience during your summer job
    c.   an interesting event that occurred during your vacation
    d.   interesting facts about your home, community or region

2.   Work Experiences

    a.   interesting jobs that you have had
    b.   interesting lessons that you have learned from your work
    c.   interesting job-related procedures that save time

3.   Beliefs

    a.   social issues (i.e., capital punishment, abortion, birth control, treatment of elderly)
    b.   economic issues (i.e., trade deficit, farming conditions, hunger in the U.S., deregulation)
    c.   political issues (i.e., relations with the Soviet Union, nuclear waste, voter turnout, tax reform, "Star Wars")

4.   Hobbies

    a.   sports
    b.   music
    c.   collections
    d.   outdoor recreation

5.   Travel

    a.   interesting places that you have been
    b.   interesting places that you would like to visit

6.   Educational Experiences

    a.   the most interesting teacher
    b.   the most rewarding course

7.   Recent Inventions and Discoveries

      a.   heart transplants
      b.   cancer research
      c.   computer maps in automobiles

After you have compiled your list of potential topics, examine the list and select the one topic that interests you the most. Then answer the following questions:

1.   Will the members of my audience be interested in the subject?

      a.   Will my topic help the members of my audience gain new insights?
      b.   Can I make the topic particularly meaningful to the members of my audience?

2.   Is my subject appropriate for this speaking occasion?

If you respond "yes" to each of these questions, you are ready to proceed to the next phase of speech preparation.

FORMULATING THE PURPOSE AND THESIS STATEMENT

Formulating your purpose includes three tasks. In this section, we will discuss the general purpose, specific purpose and thesis statement.

General Purpose

After determining your speech topic, the second step in preparing your speech is to identify the general purpose. Usually the general purpose can be placed into one of two categories: to inform or to persuade. There is a third category--to entertain, but classroom speeches are rarely of this type.

The ultimate goals of a speech to inform are to convey information and to heighten retention by the audience. Although all types of speeches contain informational materials, only the speech to inform has, as its sole purpose, to impart knowledge, to make ideas clear, and to enhance understanding.

While it is desirable that the listeners remember the important ideas of any speech, retention of information is the ultimate requirement of the informative speaker. In informative speaking, you become a "teacher" who identifies the speech topic and supporting materials with the interests, desires, and needs of the listeners. If this is accomplished, the listeners are encouraged to want to learn and to remember the information that you present.

As a persuasive speaker, your aim is to induce the audience to think, feel, or act in the manner that you desire. Although the speech to persuade might contain much informational material, such content is only a means to an end--persuasion. The persuasive speaker is an advocate who wishes the audience to take a position on the information presented.

In your speech class, the general purposes of your speeches will generally be specified for each speaking assignment. However, for speaking assignments outside the classroom, you will most often determine the general purpose of your speech. Usually this task is quite easy. Simply ask yourself. "Do I want to explain, report, or demonstrate something?" If so, your general purpose is to inform. On the other hand, if you wish to establish acceptance or to motivate action, your general purpose is to persuade.

Specific Purpose

Once you have selected your topic and identified the general purpose, the next step is to identify the specific purpose of your speech. The specific purpose statement is an infinitive sentence that tells exactly what you want your speech to accomplish. The specific purpose statement is not stated word for word in the actual speech, but is used to help you be focused as a speaker.

By stating your specific purpose, you will have started the process of synthesis--of getting organized. The specific purpose should state your personal intention--why you are going to give this presentation. Also, the statement should identify what results you expect at the end of the speech. By writing down the specific purpose, you will be able to detect problems in what you are trying to accomplish, making possible the correction of problems during the preparation of the speech rather than during the presentation.

Perhaps an example will best illustrate the process of choosing a specific purpose. Margaret Watkins has decided to give her first speech on a topic from her personal experience. She has just completed an internship in the office of a United States Senator in Washington, D. C. So, she plans to speak about what it is like to be a member of a senator's staff. This gives her a topic and a general purpose:

Topic: United States Senate internships
General Purpose: To inform

So far, Margaret has a good beginning, but now she must determine what aspect of her internship experience will be the specific focus of her speech. The differences among senators? How a bill becomes law? How the U. S. Senate is organized? Since she has only five minutes in which to present her speech, she decides to give a behind-the-scenes view of the daily routine of a Senate intern. She then states her specific purpose this way:

Specific Purpose: To inform my audience about a typical day in the life of a U.S. Senate intern.

Writing your specific purpose statement is the most important early step in preparing your speech. To further assist you in formulating the specific purpose statement, follow the guidelines listed below:

1. The specific purpose should be written as a full infinitive phrase, not as a fragment.
2. The specific purpose should be expressed as a direct statement, not as a question.
3. The specific purpose should be precise, not too vague or too general (Lucas, 1983, pp. 50-53).

At this point in the speech preparation process, you have narrowed your topic enough to begin collecting information and materials that will be used to explain and support your specific purpose. You are now ready to prepare your thesis statement.

Thesis Statement

The specific purpose statement focuses on what you want to accomplish by delivering your speech. The thesis statement concisely tells you what you want to say and is often spoken to your audience. It contains more specific information than the specific purpose and is usually formulated later in the speech preparation process, after you have completed research on your topic. It tells you the one idea that you want your audience to remember after they have forgotten everything else that you have said--the "residual message" (Lucas, p. 5).

For an example of a thesis statement, let us return to Margaret Watkins and her experience as a Senate intern. The thesis statement for Margaret Watkins' speech might be worded like this:

Thesis Statement: During a typical day, a U. S. Senate intern must accomplish three major tasks.

How will you know whether the thesis statement is well-worded? Apply the same criteria to your thesis statement that you did to your specific purpose. The thesis statement should be written as a complete sentence, should not be in the form of a question, and should not be too vague or too general. A well-worded thesis statement will result in a sharper focus and a tighter, more coherent speech.

DEVELOPING THE INTRODUCTION, BODY, AND CONCLUSION

In order to insure a logical sequencing of ideas in your speech, you must gain command of the three basic parts of a speech--the introduction, the body, and the conclusion. To understand the strategic role of each of these parts of a speech, let us examine them in the order in which you would prepare them. You begin by organizing the body of the speech, because it is impossible to know the best way to introduce your content before you have decided what the content will be.

Body of Speech

During, or immediately following, the process of gathering material for your speech, you should prepare the basic framework for the major segment of the speech--the body. The necessity for good organization in the body is apparent when you consider that it usually occupies approximately 80 to 85 percent of the total speech, whereas, the introduction perhaps averages about 10 percent and the conclusion about 5 percent.

Organizing the body of your speech begins by determining the major ideas that you wish to communicate. In selecting the "main headings," the first step is to write down all of the potential, different points that you could present in your speech. This process might begin during or after gathering the material for your speech. Your list might number ten, twenty, or even thirty separate items. Perhaps you remember when you received a jigsaw puzzle and you spread the pieces on the kitchen table. Your task was then to fit the individual pieces together to reveal the intended picture. In a sense, your list of potential main headings represents possible "pieces" of your speech body; by the process of synthesis, you must select the appropriate pieces, develop others if necessary, and fit the pieces together in appropriate positions. To illustrate, let us assume that you want to deliver a speech on the major components of the conclusion of a speech. Your list of potential main headings might look like this:

1. avoid cuteness in the conclusion
2. a restatement of your thesis statement
3. provide logical closure
4. a summary of the main ideas in the speech body
5. a reminder about why the information is important to the
    listeners
6. occasionally some references for further information
7. reestablish the connection of the topic to a larger context
8. make an appeal
9. use a striking quotation
10. do not be long-winded
11. avoid off-color humor
12. mention common relationships, beliefs, and interests
13. use a striking question
14. refer to the speech occasion
15. do not apologize

The second step in selecting your main headings is to formulate
from your list of potential main headings a group of two to five
major ideas under which you can arrange your pertinent supporting
material. As you carefully study the completed list, it will
gradually lose its jumbled appearance and a meaningful pattern of
thoughts will begin to emerge. The ideas which seem most important
to support your thesis statement will be the main points or headings
of the speech Body. Remember that several points might be
consolidated under a more general heading which is not present on
your original list. Using the list on the major components of the
speech conclusion cited above, the main headings are illustrated as
follows:

    General Purpose: To inform

    Specific Purpose: To inform the audience about major
                        components in the conclusion of a speech.

    Thesis Statement: The conclusion of a speech should contain
                        three important components.
    Body

      I.   The speaker should design the conclusion to reinforce the
            thesis statement.
     II.   The speaker should design the conclusion to summarize the
            main points in the body of the speech.
    III.   The speaker should design the conclusion to end the speech
            on a high point of interest.

In this example, the body has three main headings. Even though
the general rule states that the body of a speech should have

between two to five major headings, rarely will you have time to completely develop more than three main ideas during your classroom speeches. However, regardless of how long a speech might run, if you have too many main headings, the audience will have trouble sorting them out.

Once you establish your main headings, you need to determine the sequence in which you will present them in your speech. This is extremely important, for it will affect the clarity, retention, and possibly the persuasiveness of your ideas. Here let us examine briefly the five basic organization patterns used most often by public speakers.

Time Patterns

Arrangement, according to periods of time, is one of the frequently used patterns of organization. The time pattern is a natural method for describing a process or giving directions. In such a speech you are explaining an operation which in reality follows a time order.

Example of Time Pattern

Specific Purpose: To inform the audience about how a bill becomes law.

Body
I.   During the first step, a legislator submits the bill for consideration.
II.   During the second step, the bill is sent to the appropriate legislative committee.
III. If the committee votes for the bill, the third step involves consideration of the bill by the legislature.

In using the time pattern, you need not always maintain the chronological order. The reverse of the chronological order would equally represent a time relation, or you might start with one period of time and move to what comes before that time and then to what comes after.

Spatial Patterns

A spatial pattern for organization is a description of the subject according to the physical or geographical space that it occupies. In a spatially ordered development, you proceed from top to bottom, from bottom to top, from right to left, or from left to right.

Example of Spatial Pattern

Specific Purpose: To inform the audience about the increase of crime in the United States.

Body
I.   Increase of crime in the Eastern United States
II.   Increase of crime in the Central United States
III. Increase of crime in the Western United States

Topical Patterns

The topical ordering of main headings in the speech body is the most frequently used speech pattern. It is also the most difficult in that you cannot rely on a predetermined structure. "Some [people] say topical patterns are those which arise from the subject matter, that these are patterns evolving out of the 'natural parts' of a subject, its aspects, types, or qualities" (Wilson & Arnold, p. 176). For instance, the broad divisions of the Federal Government are based on three functions--executive, legislative, and judicial. A division of college students, according to well-known catagories, might include freshmen, sophomores, juniors, and seniors. Well-known categories are advantageous because audiences are generally more receptive to ideas that they can associate with their present knowledge.

Example of Topical Pattern

Specific Purpose: To persuade the audience that capital punishment should be abolished.

Body
I.   Capital punishment does not deter crime.
II.   Capital punishment is ultimately more costly than life imprisonment.
III. Capital punishment could conceivably be responsible for the death of innocent people.

Problem-Solution Patterns

The problem-solution pattern describes what is wrong and proposes a way to make the situation better. It is usually divided into two distinct main headings: the recognition of the problem and a solution of the problem.

Example of Problem-Solution Pattern

Specific Purpose: To persuade the audience that child abuse is
                   increasing and it must be stopped.

Body
I.   The problems of child abuse is increasing in three areas:
     a. Physical abuse
     b. Mental abuse
     c. Sexual abuse

II. The solution to these problems involves using two
     significant methods:
     a. Educational methods
     b. Legal methods

Cause-Effect Patterns

Occasionally, in speaking, the most effective method of arranging the main headings of the speech body is the use of causal relationship. Such a pattern may proceed from the cause to the effect (results), or from the effect to the cause. In using this sequence, be sure that the incidents, events, or factors which you allege to have produced a particular result have actually exerted a causal influence. You must not assume that merely because one thing follows another in time, the preceding happening causes the latter. You must argue that the causal relationship does, in fact, exist.

Example of Cause-Effect Pattern

Specific Purpose: To inform the audience about the causes of
                   inflation and its effects.

Body
I.   Inflation is caused by two major factors:
     A. Government budget deficits
     B. Increase in money supply

II. The effects of inflation have a great impact in two areas:
     A. Rising prices
     B. Rising wages

A variation of this pattern is reversing the order and presenting the effects first and then the causes. Effect-to-cause patterns would work well with a topic such as "decreasing gasoline prices; " the audience would presumably already be interested in the effects, and discussing them first, might heighten interest in your analysis of the causes.

All five of these typical organizational patterns can be used for both informative and persuasive speeches. As a general rule, however, the time and spatial patterns are most frequently used for information-type speeches, while problem-solution and cause-effect patterns are most useful for persuasive speaking. The topical pattern defies categorization and is used equally well for both informative and persuasive speeches.

As you begin to finalize the sequencing of your main headings in your speech body, try to follow these guidelines:

1. Divide your speech body into a few major headings of equal importance.
2. Have at least two, but not more than, five major headings in the speech body. (Remember that in a shorter speech, you need fewer major headings.)
3. Select major headings that are mutually exclusive.
4. Select main headings that are of equal importance to the specific purpose and thesis sentence of your speech.
5. Phrase main headings in clear language, using a consistent pattern of wording throughout (Sprague & Stuart,pp. 73--86).

After your main headings are set, you must now begin to focus on the subpoints that support your main headings. These subpoints also need to be arranged in some effective pattern--topical, spatial, whatever. However, you do not have to repeat the same pattern used for the main headings. You choose the pattern that is the most logical for each set of subpoints. The arrangement of the subpoints, in relation to the main points, is illustrated in the following example:

BODY

_____I.   Crime is increasing in the Eastern U.S.

_____ A.   Assaults are increasing.

Spatial   Topical   B.   Murders are increasing.

_____ C.   Burglaries are increasing.

_____II.   Crime is increasing in the Western U.S.

_____A.   In   1970,   crime   statistics
                        indicated. . .

Time

_____B.   In   1986,   crime   statistics
                        indicate. . .

Introduction of Speech

Beginning speakers often mistakenly begin the preparation of their speeches with the introduction. As mentioned earlier in this chapter, it is more effective to prepare the introduction after you have completed the body of your speech. That way, you know precisely what you are going to introduce. Even though it constitutes only about ten percent of your entire speech, the introduction is perhaps the most important part of your presentation. The main purposes of the introduction are to get members of the audience to focus on you as the speaker and to orient the audience to your message--your speech topic. Remember that your speech really starts before you utter the first words and that those first words are crucial to the success of your speech. As soon as the attention shifts to you, you need to begin to develop rapport and prepare the audience to listen to you. Initially, you will experience some tension because you realize how important these first moments are. Therefore, you will have to plan the introduction very carefully.

An effective introduction will accomplish four objectives: (1) gain the audience's attention, (2) announce the topic of the speech, (3) provide a psychological orientation by establishing credibility and good will, and (4) preview the main headings in the body of your speech (Lucas, pp. 159-168). Let us examine each of these objectives in turn.

Gaining the Audience's Attention.

As you begin your speech, your audience will have many
other thoughts on their minds. Your first responsibility will be to
eleminate those distractions and help the audience members focus on
what you have to say. There are several ways to gain favorable
attention. Here is a list of attention-getters:

Use a Quotation.   Quotations sometimes have a precise,
memorable wording that would be difficult for you to
duplicate. Also, they permit you to borrow from the
credibility of the quoted source. For example, a student used
the following quotation by Upton Sinclair to introduce her
speech on the need for strong pure food legislation:

There was never the least attention paid to what was cut up
for sausage. . . . Meat that had tumbled out on the floor
in the dirt and (the) sawdust. The water would drip over
it, and. . .rats would race about. . .it. The rats were
nuisances, (so) the packers would put poisoned bread out
for them, they would die, and the rats, bread, and meat
would go into the hoppers together. . . . (Interstate
Oratorical Association, 1985, p. 19).

Use an Anecdote.   A story might stimulate the audience's
interest because it shows the human side of what might
otherwise be dry, boring information.

At first Donna Alexander didn't notice the signs. Her
four-year-old son, Danny, was a bit quieter than usual,
that was all. She saw no physical signs that would cause
concern. Donna was a single mother who had to have a job
or go on welfare; it was that simple. And that complicated
matters, because she had Danny. She had been so grateful
to find a place to leave him during the day and he had
seemed to like it there. . .at first. Then gradually,
Danny became withdrawn. One day the dam burst, and Donna
felt numb as her son began to tell unbelievable stories of
neglect and abuse he suffered at the Happy Hills Day Care
Center (Interstate Oratorical Association, 1985, p. 1).

Ask a Question. A frequently employed method of creating involuntary attention in the introduction is to use a striking, brief, relevant rhetorical question. A rhetorical question causes your audience to think rather than to answer out loud.

What do Stride-Ride Shoes, the Campbell Soup Company and the Fox Chase Medical Center have in common? (Interstate Oratorical Association, 1985, p. 82).

Were you aware that hot atoms have one hundred times the temperature of the sun, and that the gulf stream changes in size and course by as much as twenty miles a day? And, that the fifteen-year Philadelphia Neoplasm Research Project has just stated that every one of 92 men who developed lung cancer since 1951 smoked, but none of the 806 observed nonsmokers developed cancer in the same period? And it's probably true that one hundred percent of the smoking people who hear this statement will not alter their opinions in any way (Interstate Oratorical Association, 1967, p. 58).

Are you a precessionary caterpillar? (Interstate Oratorical Association, 1967, p. 84).

Arouse the Audience's Curiosity. Holding the audience in suspense will heighten their curiosity and get them to wonder what your speech topic is.

A new game is sweeping the country. Anyone who wants to play can. This game has many possibilities: you could play three-dimensional tic-tac-toe, or create a new identity, or destroy someone's credit, or embezzle money, or, as in last summer's hit movie, "War Games," you could play "global-thermonuclear war." The rules? None. The penalties? Few. The playing area? Every computer in the world.
The name of this game? Unauthorized computer accessing (Interstate Oratorical Association, 1984, p. 95).

Cite a Startling Fact or Opinion. A statement that surprises an audience will make them sit up and listen.

Like most of us, Wilma Manuel dreaded painful visits to the dentist. However, after one visit to her family

dentist four years ago, she doesn't fear pain anymore.
She can't. Because her dentist did not properly monitor
her general anesthesia, she suffered irreversible brain
damage during a simple tooth extraction (Interstate
Oratorical Association, 1984, p. 21).

<u>Refer to the Audience</u>. A reference to the audience is
especially effective if it is complimentary, such as, "It is
great to have the opportunity to address a group of Colorado's
brightest young scholars."

<u>Refer to the Occasion</u>. A reference to the occasion is one way
to show your listeners that you are not giving a "canned"
speech. Lieutenant Governor Nancy Dick of Colorado began her
speech to the Colorado Association of Soil Conservation
Districts by saying,

>   I'm very happy to be here at this, your 35th annual
> state meeting. A tremendous amount has happened to
> agriculture in that time period--and you've been a major
> part of it.
>   I don't think anyone would question that Colorado is
> a great place to live. That's why I'm here and I'm sure
> that's why most of you have chosen to be here too. We
> have some of the most beautiful country in the nation;
> and a relaxed and easy lifestyle--a good place to raise
> a family.
>   Unfortunately, many of those reasons why I came here
> are the same reasons why, for instance, the Front Range
> Area from Fort Collins to Pueblo has grown 140% since
> 1950. And one has to ask "What effect has this kind of
> growth had on our state?"

Since the first words that you utter will set the mood and
tenor of your entire speech, you should write out the entire
attention-getter and then memorize it. This approach will
insure that you know exactly what you are going to say at the
beginning of your speech and will increase your self
confidence. Additional suggestions by Sprague and Stuart might
assist you in avoiding some introduction pitfalls:

Don't begin with, "Before I start I'd like to say. . ."

Don't ever begin with an apology like: "I'm not really
prepared" or "I don't know much about this, but. . ."

Don't be dramatic to the point of assuming a whole new identity or persona.

Don't use an attention-getter that has no real link to your topic.

Don't make your introduction disproportionately long.

Don't use stock phrases like "Unaccustomed as I am to public speaking."

Don't name-drop in building your credibility.

Don't startle your audience by coming out of a yoga-like trance into an explosion of oral energy (pp. 112-113).

Announcing the Thesis Statement of the Speech

If the beginning of your speech--the attention-getter--is chosen wisely, your effort to secure favorable attention will also serve to orient the listeners to the subject matter of your speech. To enable the listeners to understand the body with ease, you need to explicitly state your thesis statement. In this way, at the outset you enable the listeners to grasp the essential point or position that you will develop later. In phrasing your thesis statement avoid using sentences such as "I want to talk to you about. . ." or "My specific purpose is to inform you about. . ." Better thesis statements might be "I'm going to ask you to consider. . ." or "For the next few minutes, I will examine. . ." or "Let's explore. . ."

In addition to announcing your thesis statement, it might be necessary to present some background information on the topic at this point in your introduction. This background information often develops out of a speaker's sense of what is important and significant to both the speaker and the audience. The speaker is led to use background material when it meaningfully explains the speaker's purpose or when it illustrates the speaker's stand on a problem. For example, if there is need to define specific terms or present a bit of history about the topic, this might be the most appropriate place to interject background information. However, the background sketch can be placed in the introduction wherever it will fit in easily and logically.

Establishing Credibility and Goodwill

The credibility of a speaker focuses on the speaker's qualifications to speak on a particular topic. "The speaker's credibility need not be based on firsthand knowledge or experience. It can come from reading, from classes, from interviews, from friends" (Lucas, p. 166). No matter what the source of your expertise, always state from where you received your information.

Goodwill is necessary for all speeches, but is particularly important in speeches delivered to hostile audiences. To establish goodwill, you must identify with your listeners and their concerns even though you and the audience might share very different perspectives on a particular topic. Thrash and Sisco (1984) cite several useful "tools" to use in establishing goodwill:

1. References to similarities between speaker and audience. People tend to like someone who is similar to them.

2. References to your qualifications, credentials, or experience. The audience will consider such a speaker knowledgeable and, therefore, trustworthy.

3. References to the audience's needs, concerns, or characteristics. Your listeners would like to think that you are aware of their problems and interests. They want to be complimented on their good points (p. 91).

Previewing the Main Headings in the Speech Body

A well-planned introduction will usually preview the structure of a speech by telling the audience what your main headings will be. The preview tells them what to listen for and gives them an idea of what your method of organization will be. You might preview your main headings like this:

Today, let's explore this situation by first defining the problem of. . . . Second, we will investigate its effects on both. . . . Finally, we will realize what we must do to solve this problem.

In order to successfully determine solutions to this problem, we need to know exactly what is causing it. Basically there are three identifiable causes: (1). . ., (2). . ., and (3). . . .

We will examine the lack of education on three levels: secondary education, higher education and finally home and family education.

Conclusion of Speech

The conclusion, which represents your last chance to accomplish the specific purpose of your speech, must end the speech smoothly, strongly, and on a high point of interest. Even though it probably represents only five percent of your speech, the conclusion, like the introduction, is extremely important. The conclusion generally has two major functions: to reinforce the central idea and to signal the end of your speech. When constructing your conclusion, remember that "the speech's conclusion is the reverse of its introduction. The introduction first gains attention, then previews what will be said, the conclusion summarizes what has been said, then reinforces the audience's attention" (Thrash & Sisco, p. 99).

Reinforcing the Central Idea

You can review your central idea either through direct repetition of the thesis statement or by paraphrasing the thesis statement in different words. You might also review your main speech headings. You can review directly: "I discussed three main points about. . . . They are. . . ." You can also review indirectly: "I hope that you now have a clearer understanding of. . ., its definite hazards, and step which we can take to stop such hazards from arising."

Signaling the End of the Speech. Conclude your speech strongly. Sprague and Stuart emphasize the need for strong concluding statements when they said:

Making your topic fit together logically for your audience is not enough. They have to go out psychologically satisfied with your speech--you need to have touched them. When you plan your conclusion, think not only about what you want your listeners to understand and agree with, but also about how you want them to be feeling at the end of the speech (pp. 116-117).

According to Sprague and Stuart, this "psychological closure" can be accomplished by reminding the listeners how the topic affects their lives and by making a direct appeal (i.e., to act in a certain way, to change their attitudes) (pp. 117-119).

Whatever device you use to get "psychological closure," remember to end your speech with a flourish--with a "clincher" (Sprague & Stuart, p. 119). You can use any of the attention-getting devices suggested for the introduction (i.e., startling phrase, quotation, rhetorical question) to make your concluding statement(s) memorable. In fact, one way to effectively close your speech is to refer to the attention-getter that you used in your introduction and remind the listeners how it applies to the main points in your speech.

No matter what method you use to conclude your speech, make certain that the audience knows that you are finished. If you are forced to say, "That's all" or "I'm finished," your concluding statement(s) has not had its desired impact. The lesson is obvious; prepare your conclusion as carefully as you prepared your introduction.

Transitions, Signposts, and Internal Summaries

The strategies for organizing your speech mentioned so far should assist you in deciding where to place materials and ideas to enhance the overall structure of the speech. Now direct your attention to ways of signalling the main headings and parts of a speech in order that the listeners might easily grasp the progression of meaning and not be puzzled and distracted along the way.

Three devices that are used to keep the listeners posted on the speaker's progress are: transitions, signposts, and internal summaries.

Transitions

According to Dance and Zak-Dance (1986), "transitions move you from one point to another, they assist you in going forward, and they assist the audience in seeing the relationship among various points being made in the speech" (p.

126). Transitions provide a verbal bridge that your audience crosses to your next point without mentally leaping across a chasm. The following simple transitions illustrate possible ways of moving from one idea to another:

Now that I have clarified. . ., let's consider. . . .

I have given you one reason for. . ., now I want to give you. . . .

Since we have already considered that. . ., we should begin to see. . . .

But. . . is only one viewpoint. Equally important is. . . .

Now that you understand that. . ., what should you do?

Transitions tend to summarize what you have said and forecast what is to come, or they pose a statement or ask a question that causes the listeners to focus their attention on the next point.

Signposts

Like transitions, signposts are words or signals that let the audience know where you are in the speech. Oftentimes they are simply numbers--the first. . ., the second. . ., the third. . .--or a series of questions--What is the problem? What caused the problem? What can we do about the problem? Signposts are used frequently to delineate the main headings in the body of a speech, but can also be used to alert the audience to the fact that a significant point is coming up. To highlight significant points, you might use phrases such as these:

The most important point to remember. . .

This is extremely important to understand my point.

Be sure you keep this idea in mind. . .

Internal Summaries

Earlier in this chapter, previewing the main headings of your speech in the introduction and summarizing your speech's main point in the conclusion were discussed. Internal summaries, on the other hand, are generally found in the body of a speech. "Internal summaries are used when a speaker finishes a complicated or particularly important main point or set of main points. Rather than moving immediately to the next point, the speaker takes a moment to summarize the preceding point or points" (Lucas, p. 150).

When using transitions and internal summaries, they should be identified in your speech outline by labeling them and placing them in parentheses.

Outlining

Outlining your speech on paper is an indispensable step in speech preparation. A clear outline insures that your ideas will be arranged and fully supported. It also insures that you will have considered the logical relationship among ideas and the interrelationship among the three main parts of your speech--the introduction, body, and conclusion.

According to Sprague and Stuart, there are two "traps" that you can fall into while preparing your speech:

> Either [you] overestimate your preparedness or underestimate it. In the first case you might say, "I've researched this subject so much that I've got it down cold." Until you give the speech--or begin writing down your ideas--how can you be sure? Better to discover your mistakes with your pen as your only audience. In the second case you might say, "I'll never understand this topic, even though I've spent weeks in the library!" A session at the writing table could surprise you by making evident your unconscious understanding of the subject (p. 63).

Therefore, your outline becomes your "map"; if accurately drawn and followed, it should lead you to your goal--a well organized speech.

The Preparation Outline

No hard and fast rules govern outlining speeches, but conventional methods have been found helpful. These methods will be identified and briefly explained below.

1. Identify the Title of Your Speech. The title of your speech
   should consist of no more than five or six words that
   concisely encapsulates the main thrust of your speech.
   "Listen to the Children," "America's Internal Cold War,"
   "Capital Punishment in the Schools" are examples of
   effective speech titles. They are "catchy" and they are
   germane to the purpose of the speech. The speech title
   should be centered at the top of the first page of your
   outline.

2. State the General Purpose and the Specific Purpose of Your
   Speech. These purpose statements should be stated
   separately and follow the speech title on your outline, but
   come before the text of your speech. For example,

                        A Person's Best Friend

   General Purpose: To inform

   Specific Purpose: To inform my audience of the major
   categories of dog breeds.

3. Indicate the Basic Divisions of Your Speech: Introduction,
   Body, and Conclusion. Usually the names of the basic
   divisions of your speech are centered on the page. The
   placement of these divisions, by title, in your outline
   insures that you have an introduction and conclusion and
   that you are aware of what constitutes these portions of
   your speech.

4. Use a Consistent System of Symbolization and Indentation.
   Consistent use of a symbol system is essential in helping
   you to clarify relationships and in helping you to remember
   those relationships. In most outlining systems, Roman
   numerals, capital letters, and Arabic numerals are used to
   indicate main headings and subpoints. Each time a type of
   symbol occurs it signifies that the ideas identified are of
   approximately the same importance or weight. Since you will
   be working out a structure idea by idea, you should place
   only one symbol before any one idea. This serves as a
   caution against composing compound sentences containing more
   than one thought.

   Indention reveals the value assigned to each idea. Ideas
   subsidiary to other ideas should be indented under the

subsuming thought. In this way it will be easy to see that supports and amplifications are subordinate points. Consistent symbolization and indentation are represented in the following example:

I. Main Heading #1..

    A. Subpoint #1..

        1. ....

        2. ....

            a. ....

            b. ....

    B. Subpoint #2..

        1. ....

            a. ....

        2. ....

            a. ....

II. Main Heading #2..

    Etc. ....

III. Main Heading #3..

    Etc. ....

    In outlining a speech, it is acceptable to have a number 1 without a 2, or an (a) without a (b), in subordinate material, because your point might require only one detailed example to support it. Usually, however, a major, significant point requires at least two divisions of subordinate material.

5. <u>Use Only Complete Sentences in Your Outline</u>. An outline is a structure intended to display relationship of ideas clearly. Therefore, each idea stands separately within the structure of the outline. The need to reveal the

relationship of each idea to other ideas is the major argument for complete sentence outlining. If correctly constructed, sentences are expressions of complete thoughts. Be cautious of compound sentences in outlining; they contain more than one idea, making it impossible to follow the principle of one symbol, one idea.

6. Label Transitions and Internal Summaries. Transitions and internal summaries should be uniformly indicated and set off from the rest of the structure of the speech. They should be given technical labels such as "Transition" or "Internal Summary." A common practice is to treat these portions of the speech differently from the main headings or subpoints by omitting the use of symbols and by marking them off--enclosing them in parentheses. This practice shows that you have given careful attention to how you intend to move from one main heading or subpoint to another.

7. Include a Bibliography of Sources of Information. Sources of information should appear in the outline proper when the source is mentioned in the speech itself. However, more often such acknowledgements will be included at the end of the outline--following the Conclusion--as information for the speech instructor or other readers. The bibliography should contain cited references for all informational sources that you used in the preparation of your speech.

SUMMARY

Since human beings prefer some predictability--some organization, this chapter dealt with the step-by-step process of organizing a speech. This process begins with the selection of an appropriate speech topic and continues through the formulation of the general purpose, the specific purpose, and the thesis statement. The thesis is established in the introduction, developed in the body, and reviewed in the conclusion of a well-constructed speech. The introduction will also gain attention, establish goodwill and speaker credibility and preview the main headings that will follow in the body of the speech.

Organizing the body of the speech begins with a list of points that you might want to make in your speech. These points are organized according to the principles of outlining. They are organized to follow a logical pattern such as that of time, space, topical, problem-solution, and cause-effect. Transitions and internal summaries, strategically placed, make the organizational pattern apparent to the audience.

Along with reviewing your thesis and/or main headings, the conclusion helps the audience remember the ideas and signals the end of the speech.

Chapter Four

Audio-Visuals

By

Robert Ross

Audio-visuals are an appropriate medium provided they are created, selected, and utilized according to an effective plan. The design for a presentation must conform to the overall purpose for speaking. The design is a plan which facilitates the purposes of the presentation and the presenter for a specific audience and occasion. The design for audio-visuals should be aimed toward supporting and enhancing the message rather than becoming the message in and of itself.

DESIGN FOR AUDIO-VISUALS

The audio-visual design varies according to the following components: the subject of the presentation, the purpose(s) of the presenter, the audience(s) for the presentation, the occasion for the presentation, and the physical space for the presentation.

The Subject of the Presentation

Although the purpose of presentations may vary, a purposeful design for the use of audio-visuals is necessary. Thus, the creation, selection and use of aids should enhance but not replace the message. The focus is not on the aid or the speaker, but the subject of the presentation.

The Purpose of the Presenter

The purposes for the utilization of audio-visuals are varied. Audio-visuals may be utilized to increase the organizational flow of

a presentation, as a memory aid for the speaker, as a means for
presenting complex ideas which are difficult to verbalize, and as a
way to release of tension. The design for audio-visuals usually
reflects multiple purposes of the presenter.

The effective use of audio-visuals affects the speaker's
credibility as well as the original purpose for the aid. By
effectively using a single or series of overhead transparencies,
posters or flipcharts, speakers can know where they are in the
presentation. The audience perception that the speaker is in
control and organized, enhances his or her credibility. A speaker's
credibility may be reduced by improper or ineffective use of
audio-visual equipment or materials. Furthermore, the message of
the speech is affected negatively by the speaker's inept use of
audio-visuals.

A speaker who wishes to present multiple sources for emphasis
or support without verbalizing them can provide the information on a
visual graphic. The use of a visual in this instance saves time in
a brief presentation and provides multiple sources of evidence in an
appropriate format that does not bore the audience.

The design for audio-visuals is a decision-making process where
an individual's reasons for using audio-visuals are identified, the
appropriate medium is selected, and the presentational skill level
for the selected medium is perfected.

The Audience For The Presentation

The audience for a presentation includes individuals present in
the physical space during the presentation. Individuals or
audiences who may respond to the presentation after the fact through
a secondary source (e.g. press report, discussion with an audience
member present during the presentation) represent a special group.
If the secondary source is confused, or has incomplete information
on the message, the broader audience may misinterpret the
presenter's message. The use of a handout which clearly delineates
the salient points is effective in addressing these
broader audiences. Special consideration must be given to this
broader audience in the design and use of audio-visuals.

The Occasion For The Presentation

The occasion for the presentation includes special events,
ceremonies, or functions. These include things such as retirements,
school board meetings, welcome meetings for new employees, or

visitation of an honored guest or alumni. The occasion may be a regularly scheduled occurrence such as daily lectures to a class you are teaching or weekly status reports. The occasion may be a favorable opportunity or an exigency such as the availability of a knowledgeable source on a topic of interest to the group or the first board meeting following withdrawal of state funding for education. The occasion influences the design of audio-visuals. Your goal is to capture the essence of the moment and to effectively support the message.

The presenter should also incorporate the customs or expectations of the group or organization in the design of appropriate audio-visual aids. The message and the audio-visuals utilized must fit the spirit of the occasion.

The Physical Space of the Presentation

The physical space for the presentation influences the design and use of audio-visuals. Since the audio-visuals must be seen and heard by all audience members, adequate equipment must be readily available to the presenter. The necessity for pre-speech discussions with the sponsor for a speech are essential to assure access and availability of audio visual equipment.

The Speech Communication department can provide an overhead machine, a screen, chalkboard, moveable table, and an easel for displaying posters or flip charts. Additional electrical equipment you may need must be obtained from the Educational Material Service of your university. You may need to provide a minimum of two weeks advance notice for the use of this equipment.

The presenter must be seen and heard by the members of the audience. The use of appropriate lighting for different types of audio-visuals needs to be coordinated in the design. If possible, the presenter should practice the presentation in the physical space where the presentation will be given. When this is not possible, the presenter should obtain information about the space to effectively design the audio-visuals for presenting the message in that space. When speaking as part of a team of speakers, the group should organize themselves so they will effectively use the space and save time. For example, if speakers one and two need to use an overhead projector, they should be followed by speakers three and four who rearrange the space and equipment to use the chalkboard or an easel for holding a chart. The effective use of space is not only the responsibility of a single speaker but a group of presenters for a specific occasion.

The five components for design of audio-visuals are interdependent components. The physical space is usually flexible and can be changed to fit the occasion, to accommodate the expected audience size, or to allow the presenter to use a specific audio-visual aid. The audience is not static, even for a specific group. Guests are expected at a Kiwanis or Rotary luncheon. The characteristics of a specific group such as Kiwanis are a composite of individual members who are committed by various degrees to different beliefs or hold dissimilar values on specific topics. The audience members uniquely process the message delivered by the presenter. Some members primarily utilize information that is visual in form while others attend to auditory data. Each audience member judges the message, the appropriateness of the audio-visual, and the techniques of the presenter differently. The five components operate in concert, not independently. The presenter in designing the audio-visuals should recognize this interdependence.

CREATING THE SYMBOLIC MESSAGE

The act of creating the symbolic message is integrally related to the design for audio-visuals. The presenter may produce a visual message on the chalkboard or prepare a transparency, a poster or flip chart for use. The presenter may construct a model or obtain the actual object which may be touched, tasted, or smelled. The presenter may create a musical background for the presentation or tape-recorded interviews of significant authorities on the subject. The media provide the audience with sensory data, which if carefully managed, will result in a deeper awareness or understanding of the subject. All five human senses (sound, touch, sight, smell, and taste) should be considered in the creation of symbolic messages for a specific subject. An appropriate mix of sensory input is a goal of the creation phase of the design. Although the focus of this chapter is on audio-visuals, the other three senses should be considered and appealed to if appropriate for the subject.

The process of creating a symbolic message has three separate interdependent components: origination, utilization, and interpretation.

Origination

The act of origination involves any activity which results in the creation of sensory data for the audience. The origination may take the form of prepared materials (e.g. films, charts, models, tape recordings), or they may be spontaneous to the event, and result from the collaboration of the speaker and audience. For illustration consider the following examples of spontaneous and collaborative origination.

The presenter is making an argument to the City Council that the City streets need repair. Appropriately prepared materials have been created and are being presented. One of the salient points of the argument is the safety factor. "Pot holes can result in loss of control of vehicles which may result in the injury of passengers or drivers." The speaker is prepared to present statistics from insurance and police reports which provide cold hard facts. While these arguments are being presented, someone in the audience stumbles and falls as a result of a torn piece of carpeting. The experienced presenter will capitalize on this unique event in an appropriate manner to humanize the cold statistics of human suffering resulting from accidents which are caused by improper maintenance.

Trainers, professional briefers, and teachers have all experienced the result of collaboration between themselves and the audience. They can utilize the audience to illustrate a point by asking a question which requires a physical movement or some type of response. Continuing with the City Council illustration, consider the effect on the council of the audiences standing up or raising their hands to the following questions. "How many of you or your relatives have been involved in an accident as a result of improper road maintenance?" Or, "How many of you would consider voting for a candidate for the next election who will repair the streets?" These visual displays can be augmented with vocal responses. The point of these examples is that origination can be preplanned and prepared or it can be a spontaneous happening which illustrates a point, creates an environment or portrays an emotion pertinent and appropriate to the topic.

Utilization

Utilization implies judgments about the utility or suitability of the ways we employ our creations. Consider the presenter who is briefing middle managers on changes in insurance coverage for the company. The briefer turns on the overhead to display a transparency with the word "SEX" in bright red print and says, "Now that I have your attention,. . . Ha ha . . . let's talk about changes in insurance." The introduction of this visual aid is not suitable to the topic because it has little if any link to insurance coverage, except perhaps maternity coverage. The central theme of the presentation has not been supported by the visual aid, thus, its utility is limited. Utility implies usefulness, thus, when an audio-visual accomplishes multiple purposes simultaneously, its utility increases.

Utility is accomplished when the audio-visual accomplishes its purpose. A transparency, poster, or flip chart which displays the outline for the presentation (figure 1) has utility and is suitable for the formality of the meeting and the audience.

Figure 1: A Sample Visual Aid

```
┌─────────────────────────────────┐
│                                 │
│    INSURANCE COVERAGE           │
│                                 │
│    CHANGE IN POLICY             │
│                                 │
│    FORMS FOR COMPLETION         │
│                                 │
│    IMPACT OF CHANGE             │
│                                 │
└─────────────────────────────────┘
```

The visual-aid can be used both in the introduction and conclusion of the briefing. Obviously, additional visual-aids can be created for each topic of the presentation.

The way that the presenter employs audio-visuals affects the audience's comprehension of information, their acceptance of multiple sensory data, and creation of the appropriate mood or atmosphere for the topic. The presenter who tries to place too much information on a visual, stands between the visual and the audience, or removes the visual prematurely will frustrate the audience or confuse them about the topic.

Interpretation

An audio-visual usually needs to be introduced, utilized and then interpreted. The interpretation process is an opportunity to bring out the meaning, or minimally to indicate one's particular conception, of the data. Presenters need to be cautious not to offend the audience by interpreting every facet of the data. It is especially important not to slant the interpretation of data in one direction when other interpretations are reasonable. However, the presenter has the responsibility to interpret the data from his or her point of view.

To illustrate the interdependence of origination, utilization and interpretation consider this example: A department head or project director effectively presents a series of audio-visuals on the dimensions of the problem, the data impacting on the issue, and proposes two options for resolving the problem. The degree of complexity of the issue, the data, and the options calls for separate, individual decisions or interpretations. If complexity is high, a series of interpretations followed by an audio-visual summary should be presented. As the quantity of data increases, the need for interpretation increases. The interpretation phase is essential to the effective creation and utilization of an audio-visual aid.

The skill of interpretation commences with the introduction of the verbal or visual supporting material, continues while presenting the visual, and is culminated in the conclusion for each audio or visual aid. The degree of interpretation required for each audience member will vary. Thus, the presenter must strive for a high degree of clarity and understanding in the introduction, presentation, and conclusion. The best method for judging how much interpretation is needed is to practice the presentation before a sample audience similar to the target audience. Afterward, an honest discussion of their interpretation will be helpful.

AUDIO-VISUAL MEDIA

Audio-visuals are available in several forms but collectively they function to support the reason for speaking. Audio-visuals can be an aid to the speaker and the audience by making a point, reinforcing or clarifying meaning, increasing retention, defining or identifying, focusing attention, or generating a mood.

During the preparation of audio-visuals, the speaker should remember to check for visibility, audibility, clarity and simplicity in the finished aid. Visibility means that all audience members can see everything that is on the visual aid. Audibility means that all audience members can hear the sound. Clarity means the visual design can be understood at first glance or that the sound of an audio is clear of electronic interference or other noise sources. Simplicity means that the visual shows only what is essential or the auditory aid provides no more information than necessary. The audio-visual should focus attention, rather than scatter or diffuse, attention.

The discussion of media will be divided into three sections: visual, audio, and audio-visual. Each section will define the forms, provide examples of the form, describe the support equipment for display of the form, and discuss the effective utilization of the form and equipment.

Visual Media

In this section, we will discuss principles and types of visual aids. The preparation and selection of visual materials and equipment must be followed by a design for their appropriate use. The decision on equipment and display is influenced by several variables including: the degree of formality desired, the availability and mobility of equipment, the size of the audience, and the presenter's skill in using the equipment. The options for selection and use are numerous but should be carefully chosen to address all the variables.

Charts, Maps, Graphs

The organization of content for display in the forms of graphs, maps, or charts involves specific decisions. Several forms of display are available and displayed in newspapers and magazines you read daily, in the textbooks of a current class, and by professors lecturing.

The format of a graph may illustrate the relationships of parts to the whole, as in a bar graph or divided circle graph. For example, every organization has a flow chart or line chart which illustrates the direction of movement, the division of employees, or the level for appropriate decision making. In a basic geography class you were introduced to both topography and spatial maps. Several times in dreaming about owning a home or buying a car you have viewed a pictograph or seen a dissection of how that car engine looks inside. The display of information to enhance the message can be designed in many forms of graphs, maps or charts. The specific form must be consistent with the visual medium utilized. Since charts are very common in classroom speaking, we will devote more attention to types of charts.

Charts are an effective means of sharing information. They can be prepared in advance or constructed during the briefing to visually portray audience responses. Material prepared in advance of the presentation is expected by most audiences.

Constructing a chart should commence with a design layout on a piece of blank 8 1/2" X 11" piece of paper or newsprint. Initially you should construct the chart in pencil to determine the symmetry of your material and to eliminate information not essential to the final chart. This initial chart is constructed in three steps.

First, determine the key concepts you wish to present. Second, identify the specific word(s) which best portrays the limited number of key concepts. Third, order or sequence the specific words representing the key concepts in a meaningful pattern.

After you have constructed the initial chart, the final presentational chart should be constructed using some basic principles for effective design. Some of these principles are:

- Legibility is best when letter size is larger than one inch.
- The number of words on the chart should be fewer than twenty-five.
- Bold print or underlining is used to draw attention to main ideas. Thinner lines and smaller print are used for details or subpoints.
- Color is utilized appropriately. Normally dark colors are utilized for visibility and clarity with contrasting, bright colors (e.g. red, orange) to underline or outline material.

Charts are appropriate for a formal or informal presentation although the addition of special lighting may be required to enhance visibility. Charts and newsprint are limited in utility for audiences who cannot be seated within 20 to 40 feet of the display. With the exception of an easel or some other display device, no special equipment is required for their use.

The presenter should move to the chart and stand to one side while interpreting the chart. When referring to a specific point on the chart, the presenter should use a pointer and hold it in position for no fewer than 3 seconds. Assessment of the audience's nonverbal expressions may indicate the desire for questions about the chart's content. The presenter should spend enough time on the chart to ensure understanding of its content and significance to the speaker's topic. The decision to leave the chart exposed after discussion depends upon the nature of the content. Unless the chart is organizational in nature, you should remove or cover the chart since you need the attention of the audience when shifting to a new source of support or to a different component of the speech.

Remember for charts:

- Position the material so everyone can see it.
- Print legibly and large when constructing the chart.
- Don't block the audience's view.
- Remove or cover when not in use.
- Use a pointer or your entire hand in focusing attention.
- Chart size must fit your audience size.

      -   Allow the audience time to view the chart.
      -   Interpret the chart's significance to your topic.

A chart card is the most expensive form of chart since the information is mounted or prepared on a posterboard or heavy cardboard. The advantage is that the material is sturdy enough to be displayed on an easel, on a table leaning against the podium, on the tray of a chalkboard, or mounted on the wall.

A flip chart is usually a 28" x 34" pad of paper for displaying information. The information presented is usually prepared in advance of the presentation. The material is inexpensive and may be displayed on an easel, leaning against a podium or pages detached from the pad mounted on the wall. Since the visibility of most material presented on a flip chart or chart card is limited to 20 to 40 feet, these options should be considered for only small audiences.

Chalkboards

Most presentational areas have a permanent or moveable chalkboard available for presenting information. Information can sometimes be placed on the chalkboard in advance, as it becomes appropriate to the topic, or when generated by the audience. The chalkboard is most appropriately utilized to review information generated through interaction between the speaker and audience. A trainer, teacher and skilled briefer will either plan for audience input as part of the presentation or sense that a point needs further clarification for the audience. Use of the chalkboard to add clarification or to display audience responses establishes clear links among the audience, topic, and presenter. The chalkboard can also be used to present information that does not lend itself to a transparency or chart.

When using a chalkboard, some of the following visual principles need to be followed:

      -   Erase all unrelated material.
      -   Check lighting to avoid glare.
      -   Print legibly and neatly with letters 2 to 3 inches high.
      -   Leave sufficient space between lines.
      -   Limit information to key words or phrases.
      -   Use colored chalk or underlining for emphasis.
      -   And especially, break chalk in half if it squeaks.

The presenter needs to use effective skills when referring to the material on the chalkboard:

- Use a pointer to focus audience attention.
- Place the material on the board and then stand to the side so the audience can see the material.
- Don't speak to the chalkboard, maintain audience contact.
- Move to another location in the room or erase the material on the chalkboard when shifting topics.
- Summarize the material and interpret its significance to your speech topic.

The chalkboard provides the presenter with an opportunity to involve the audience in generating information, allows for immediate clarity and expansion of information on a topic and for release of energy in movement by the presenter. The chalkboard is messy to use, has limited visibility for the audience, and requires skill for effective use. Unless the availability of equipment or preparation time precludes the use of prepared charts, transparencies, or slides, the chalkboard should be reserved for spontaneous extension of information or for recording audience responses to presenter questions.

For illustration, consider a meeting of an organized group (e.g., teacher's union, staff of a department) that is attempting to clarify their objectives for the next year or to implement a previously agreed upon goal. The presenter has outlined clearly the need for the objectives, provided extensive information that documents the variables to be considered for implementation, and stimulated the audience to want to participate in the decision for the group. The presenter provides the appropriate transition for the audience to shift from a recipient of information to a generator of information. The presenter then shifts to a role of recorder of ideas and later to that of analyzer and synthesizer of information generated by the audience. The chalkboard is an appropriate visual medium for planned audience participation or spontaneous extension and clarification of information.

Remember, when using the chalkboard:

- Print legibly and neatly.
- Allow the audience to review the material prior to interpretation.
- Erase information when no longer needed.
- Practice using the chalkboard until your skill level is proficient.

Objects

Actual Objects

Unless the actual object is too small or large, cumbersome, or uncontrollable, the presenter may want to display the actual object. The use of objects can be effective for illustrating specific points in a presentation. However, the presenter should always consider the safety of the audience and the psychological state which may be created when you become too dramatic. Let me cite two student speeches as examples. The first student speech was on reptiles and the speech was excellent up to a point. When the rather large snake got out of the bag, a portion of the audience started to panic. The second example was also an excellent speech focusing on a new product which extinguishes fire in a matter of seconds. The demonstration was successful, but the resulting fumes forced evacuation of the room. I was personally surprised when the water sprinkler system did not activate. Both students followed the rule of obtaining permission from the professor for utilizing the object and demonstrating the product. My decision next time will be different.

Models

A display which portrays a prototype of an object can be used instead of the actual object. Some models are intricate enough to demonstrate the operation of the product.

A working model is designed with movable parts. For illustration, consider the office manager who brings in a scale model of the physical office space with moveable objects representing desks, file cabinets, etc. and as part of the total presentation asks their assistance in designing a functional environment. Provided the need for change is documented and acknowledged, the working model will provide viable options for group or management decision. This working model can be combined with pictures from an instant camera to illustrate the final product.

Exhibits or display boards

These can be prepared in advance to supplement the specific presentation or to provide additional materials which are related to a broader topic. For example, the representative from personnel who is presenting a speech on insurance benefits for employees can have a display board with information handouts on other topics (e.g.

retirement, investment plans). You are not expected to consider this approach for your first course in public speaking.

The advantage of using objects, models or exhibits is the arousal of other senses; tactile, olfactory, taste. Audience involvement and participation can be enhanced with the effective utilization of these visual media providing the object is amenable to and suitable for handling. The presenter who is exhibiting the various stages of constructing a stained glass window had best alert the audience that some objects are not suitable for handling lest the presenter desires more pieces than was originally called for in the design. A series of models of proposed buildings can be effective in displaying an architectural design. A working model is a useful form for audience participation.

Experts

People are objects too and as such can be utilized in a presentation. This requires special consideration so that your presence is still necessary and appropriate. Several questions should be raised in considering this option. For example, is this person truly an expert? If the answer is affirmative, then you need to negotiate their availability, how long they will speak and how you will coordinate their introduction and the transition back to yourself.

The use of experts changes the role of the originator of the topic from the prime speaker to a secondary role. For the first course in public speaking the use of experts should be relegated to audio tape recorded interviews so that you can remain in control and be the primary speaker.

Another method in using others is in the role of resource person. When presenting a demonstration, resource persons other than classmates will be beneficial. The major advantage of utilizing outsiders is you can train them and practice to perfection their specific role. When using others remember you are the primary speaker and thus you need to control and effectively coordinate other's behaviors to enhance your performance. No one needs another to "steal the spotlight."

Remember, for objects, models, exhibits and experts:

- Select those that provide clarity and dimension for the topic.
- Place the object so that the audience can view it directly.
- Don't select them if you cannot be in control.

- Audience involvement can be enhanced with effective use.
- Utilize additional presenters or experts for assistance when necessary.
- Move away from, or cover the specimen, model or exhibit when you wish to change topics.
- Allow enough time for the audience to experience the specimen, model or exhibit.
- Interpret the material for your purpose in speaking.

Visual Projecting Equipment

This equipment includes things like the transparency projector, opaque projector, filmstrip projector, and computer assisted graphics, etc. In this section we will discuss some of the more familiar ones.

Transparencies and Overhead Projectors

These devices are popular means of displaying information. Transparencies result from a photograph of prepared or selected materials which are transposed on acetate in a black/white contrast by most copying machines. You can also draw on a blank transparency with special pens to create a visual during a presentation. Information presented on a blank acetate is less professional and therefore is not recommended. The material can be displayed on a screen or a light colored wall. Transparencies are inexpensive to produce, easily stored, mobile, and durable. Transparencies can be produced from created materials or materials selected from other sources (e.g. textbooks, pictures and maps). Transparencies can be a single sheet or multiple overlays.

In construction of a transparency for your speech some basic principles should be followed. First, determine the basic ideas to be presented from the original source. For example, if you want to display statistics from a research report, determine if the print size from the original document is large enough to produce a transparency directly. If the material is less than 1/4 inch or the material is cluttered, then type the material to provide clarity and simplicity of design for producing a transparency. Transparencies should normally be limited to fifteen to twenty words and the print size should be primary type not elite or pica type. Complex ideas should be broken down into segments and presented one at a time. The transparency should focus attention on key ideas.

The projector can be used with room lights on and can be operated by the presenter. This type of display material is suitable for either a formal or informal occasion and can be viewed by a large audience with proper magnification. It requires the equipment and skill in delivery for effective use. If you are operating the overhead, place the machine on a moveable stand or table so the audience can see the projection. The transparency should fill the screen.

The person operating the machine while speaking needs to maintain eye contact with the audience. The presenter can turn on the machine, check for needed focus and then shift away from the machine to interpret the material. The presenter may utilize a pencil or pen to lay on the transparency to focus the audience's attention to specific items. Items on the transparency can be masked with a piece of paper until you are ready to project the image. When you are finished utilizing the overhead, turn off the machine and return to another part of the presentation arena in front of the audience prior to continuing your presentation.

Remember, for transparencies:

- Almost anything can become a transparency.
- Adjust the projector's mirror so the image fills the screen.
- Have transparencies in coordinated order with speech.
- Focus the image or check the focus for each transparency.
- Position yourself to interpret the material and not block the audience's view.
- Show only the part of the transparency you are talking about.
- Turn off the machine between transparencies or when finished.

Opaque Projectors

This devise is useful for presenting an image of material which cannot be effectively presented by a slide or transparency. Currently, opaque projectors are large, noisy, and of minimal quality in visual projection. Although the opaque projector has drawbacks, it should be considered as an option when information needs to be shared with large audiences. The image projected on a screen or wall can easily be viewed by 20 to 60 audience members.

Slide Projectors

Slide projectors are used to display 35 mm slides. The advantage of slides includes the addition of much more detail, including color and natural environments, than is possible in a single photograph. An entire audience, from one individual to sixty, can see the display simultaneously. The use of slides is appropriate for a formal or informal presentation and requires only the skill of using a projector. The projector can be controlled from the front of the room. When interpreting slides, the presenter should stand to one side of the screen so the audience can see the projected image and the speaker.

The disadvantage of slide projectors includes potential equipment malfunctioning and room darkening which decreases the focus on the presenter. The major advantage of using slides is the enriched visual imagery which can be portrayed in minute detail at minimum expense. A slide presentation can create an appropriate mood or environment for a presentation more effectively than other visuals.

Remember, for slides:

- Sequence the slides prior to the presentation.
- Coordinate lighting requirements with a colleague.
- Stand to one side of the projected image for interpretation.
- Utilize a pointer for focusing attention to detail.
- Allow the audience time to comprehend the slide.
- Coordinate audio with the visual images.
- Practice using the machine until your skills are perfected.
- Be prepared if the machine malfunctions.
- Provide an interpretation of the visual importance to the message of your speech.

Filmstrip Projector

These are useful when a process or flow of actions needs illustration. The technique is useful in presenting a sequence of events or patterns of behavior. The process requires the use of a prepared filmstrip, which may be purchased, on a topic or the original design of images which are photographed and packaged as a filmstrip. The filmstrip machine is easy to operate and the filmstrip is easily storable.

Computer Assisted Graphics

Computer assisted graphics can be generated by computers and displayed on a video screen. With the use of a printout provided as a handout these can form the content base for a slide, chart or transparency. You can use the computer to assist you in constructing graphics, printing a hard copy, and then reproducing the hard copy into a transparency, handout, slide or flip chart.

You may have access to a personal computer for designing your graphics prior to construction. University students probably have access to the software package "Print Shop" for use on the Apple Computers. A computer assisted graphics system is available in most large organizations.

If the appropriate options for computer assisted graphics are available, the presenter should experiment in generating materials which support the topic. Futuristic implications for the information base stored in a computer could result in the use of a large screen reproduction of support material as part of a presentation. Computers can generate information called for by interaction between the presenter and audience. Consider for example, a meeting of a school board where a member of the superintendent's staff is discussing the topic of enrollment projections for new curriculum proposals. A computer assisted graphic on-line link-up for the presentation would allow for immediate information on space allocation, budget projection, student records of achievement, etc., as those questions are raised covering the proposed project. Information can be displayed on a set of variables using several designs referred to earlier in this chapter (e.g., divided circle, bar graphs).

To effectively utilize on-line generated computer graphics will require the presenter to develop new skills in operation of the machine as well as shift to an impromptu speaking style for delivery during that phase of the presentation. Computer assisted graphics are with us now, but the interface of computer and presentational skills will have to be practiced in order to be effective.

Remember, for other visual projecting equipment:

-- Determine the useability of the equipment
-- Develop the skills necessary for operation of the equipment
-- Shift your presentational style to impromptu for interpretation and response to questions from the audience.

Summary

Other visual aids and projecting equipment are available from distributors or can be created with imagination. This section has described the primary visual aids and equipment used in, and available for, most presentational situations. Visual aids are selected to supplement, not to replace, the verbal message. In the selection of visual aids the presenter should consider the factors of appropriateness for the topic, skill level of the presenter, and audience acceptance of the visual aid as a means of presentation.

Commercially Prepared Visual Aids

Posters, pictures, cartoons, signs, bumper stickers, and buttons are examples of prepared visuals which can be used in a speech. These types of visuals should be carefully selected and used only when they fit the occasion, topic, and type of audience. A student presenting a speech on insurance linked a colorful poster of a chicken sitting on a partially exposed layer of eggs to his topic of security. The three by five foot poster was placed on the wall immediately behind him and referred to appropriately throughout the presentation. Posters can attract and arouse interest in the topic and are appropriate if interfaced with the theme of the presentation.

Cartoons can arouse attention and create a joyful climate. An example of effective utilization of cartoons and characterizations was at a recent dinner honoring the 60th birthday of a friend. The spirit of celebration was fellowship tempered with frivolous gifts and generally a high degree of levity. The use of cartoons was appropriate to mix effectively the degree of seriousness and levity expected by the hostess and to relieve the honoree's discomfort at being honored. Contrast this appropriate usage of cartoons with the use of cartoons in a presentation about a serious topic such as the MX missile or cancer. Only the most professional presenter can effectively deliver a satire which incorporates levity about a serious topic.

The use of pictures, unless they are posterboard in size, is usually not effective for a presentation. When you distribute small pictures in the audience you have lost the audience from further direct attention to your message. Remember, if the audience cannot see the material from their seat don't use the material.

Memorabilia in the form of bumper stickers, signs, posters, buttons, etc. can be effectively used for a presentation that is nostalgic in nature. Similarly, new material designed for promotion of a product or person can be effectively used as a visual aid. The key to its effectiveness for each event is the introduction of the item to impart significance to the object or person. The recipient must be made to feel proud, honored and delighted to receive and wear the button or to display the sign, poster, or bumper sticker. Political campaigns are an excellent arena for use of these visuals to promote a candidate. Many corporations have successfully utilized these visuals to promote a product and to motivate individuals to excel.

Remember, for commercially prepared aids:

- The object must have significance for the topic.
- The presenter must interpret the significance for the audience.
- The object must fit the occasion and mood you wish to create.
- The availability of several options (e.g., posters, bumper stickers, buttons) for selection enhances their utility for unique audience personalities.

Handouts

Handouts constitute material to be distributed prior to, during, or after the presentation. Instructional briefings or training sessions often provide participants with material to read prior to the presentation.

When using handouts, provide the material well in advance so that participants have adequate time for reading and comprehension. Don't overload the audience with extraneous information. Keep your writing concise and to the point. Include graphics, charts or diagrams that you use in your presentation as a transparency or posterboard size chart. Organize the handouts in the order of use in your presentation. Consider providing space for notes in the design of your handout. Remember to reference sources of materials you are citing. Many times a single page handout is all that is required not a booklet of materials. Refer to the material directly in your presentation but do not duplicate the content in its exactness except when talking about a specific source. A common complaint of students in classrooms is that the professor lectured from the readings and handouts provided. The handout is an aid not an exact duplicate of the presentation.

Unless you are using the handout specifically during a presentation or as an outline for the presentation, material should be distributed at the conclusion. Otherwise, most audience members will attend to the handout material as soon as they see it.

When you distribute, or have others distribute materials, pause for the recipient to scan the material prior to interpreting the information. In interpreting the material be specific but don't read what the audience has just read. If you have more than six members in the audience, ask others to distribute the information for you. A good rule of thumb is to divide the audience by six and identify that number of people to help you. For example, an audience of 30 individuals requires five assistants who are notified at the same time to distribute the materials previously given to them. All members of the audience receive the material approximately at the same time and those who read faster will not become as bored with a slow reader's scan rate.

Materials distributed during the briefing should be referred to immediately. The material must be linked to the presentation and may be followed by a brief question and answer period prior to shifting to another topic. Consider the office manager at a regularly scheduled staff meeting who is explaining how to fill out a new form. A chart, poster, drawing on the chalkboard, or transparency may be utilized by the presenter to focus attention for the entire group on a specific element of the form. When the audience has their personal copy of the form for reference, for jotting down notes, or for sample completion during the presentation, their comprehension may be enhanced.

Materials which are provided following a presentation need to be in a form that is usable and retainable. Trainers, office managers, and instructors are well aware of the filing of handouts in the "circular file" or wastebasket. Materials which are punched for easy insertion into a previously provided file folder or notebook clearly labeled are usually retained. Unless the materials are designed in a usable form for reference purposes, their usage rate may be low. An office manager who has regularly scheduled meetings on topics such as office policies, benefits, form changes, etc. would be advised to provide each employee with a separate folder or notebook binder which is brought to the meeting for immediate update by insertion of information properly prepared. The consultant/trainer should provide a training notebook for retention and referral by the trainees. The presenter needs to determine the distribution of materials and clearly state their intended usage.

Handouts can be effective but do not replace the presenter. The presenter must be in control of the distribution and the interpretation of the handout. The selection of handouts must be purposeful in design, clear in content, and supportive of the message of the presentation.

Remember, for handouts

- The material must have utility for the audience and topic.
- The material should be introduced by the presenter and given significance. Always link the material to your topic.
- The presenter should use others for distribution.
- Material should be clearly presented using concise language for the specific topic and audience.
- Refer to the handout immediately after distribution.

Audio Media

Audio media include sound systems, tape recorders, and record players. In this section we will discuss the use of each.

Sound Systems

Sound Systems are appropriate for presentations before audiences of 50 or more individuals. When speaking to some public groups (e.g., city council, school board or public forums) a sound system is used not only for amplification but for creating a public record of proceedings.

Effective use of an amplification system requires selecting the correct sound level to ensure proper volume throughout the room, while using a range of pitches and tones for speaking. Adjustment is also required to avoid electronic feedback.

When speaking to an audience, the microphone should be adjusted or attached to the speaker so that freedom of movement is not curtailed. When the presenter wishes to shift from a podium to an overhead machine, to a video replay monitor, to the chalkboard or just move about the presentational space, the sound system must accommodate these presentational shifts.

If a microphone stand is used its height should be adjusted to the speaker's height. The presenter is responsible for obtaining assistance from the host or sponsoring group to provide an appropriate amplification system. The presenter would be wise to practice the presentation in the speaking room, using the amplification system to check the system's utility and flexibility.

Remember, when using a sound system

- Adjust the volume to your speaking range.
- The sound system should allow for movement of the speaker and naturalness in delivery.
- An amplification system should enhance the auditory signal not detract from the speaker's presence.

Tape Recorders

Tape recorders are useful for providing verbal supporting evidence to a presentation and creating the appropriate mood or climate for the topic. Verbal supporting materials include expert testimony, opinions from important sources, or examples/stories appropriate for the topic. Consider for illustration, a presentation that you have prepared on the link between smoking and cancer. To quote the Surgeon General of the United States may be effective but to provide a tape recorded statement from the source is more effective. The audience has less doubt about the credibility of a speaking expert than a quoted expert. In preparation of the presentation, the speaker may have interviewed several prior smokers and wish to relate their views as support for stopping smoking. A tape recorded statement is more powerful especially if one of them is speaking through his or her larynx because mouth cancer resulted in the inability to speak normally. Another prior smoker may demonstrate in the recording a shortness of breath or some other respiratory ailment. Further documentation for the presentation may be from interviews of non-smokers describing their views of smoking. Some examples of statements I remember in one presentation included: "smokers stink," "green slimy vomit," "foul breath," and "they pollute my air!" A tape recording captured the intensity of feeling and the strength of belief that could not be demonstrated or expressed by a single presenter in representing the opinions of others. The audio recording created a mood much more effectively than the visual media alone.

Many different options are available in tape recorders. The presenter should select a machine that provides adequate amplification for the size of the audiences they will be speaking before. Some machines have the capability to become a sound system for the speaker as well as being linked to an existing sound system.

The presenter must be familiar with the operation of the machine. Adjustment of the volume for different speakers or shifting to usable portions of a lengthy interview to meet the time restraints for speaking are typical requirements for tape recorder use. The tape recorder is a viable option for most speaking occasions, topics, and audiences.

Remember, when using tape recorders:

- Consider your skill level in operating the machine.
- Create or capture the feeling level of speakers to enhance or facilitate the establishment of a mood.
- Provide the appropriate volume and clarity of content for audibility to the entire audience.
- Interpret to reinforce your message.

Record players

These are useful for presenting auditory stimuli from existing materials. The quality of sound production from tape recorders has improved to the extent that few instances occur where a record player would be required. A tape recorder is much more mobile, flexible in options and easier to operate. Tapes are more readily stored than records. Even though, for many purposes, record players are obsolete, they represent an option which should be considered by the speaker.

Auditory systems are important in many presentations. Learning theorists conclude that some individuals attend more to the audio channel for information than the visual medium. The mood or climate for a topic can be created or enhanced with the effective use of auditory stimuli.

Audio-Visual Media

Audio-visual media include the use of VCR equipment, films, and multi-media. Since our classroom speaking schedules are tight and you are allowed such a brief period of time for speaking we do not recommend your utilization of audio-visual media (e.g. multi-media, films or VCR) for the public speaking course. In other classes you may be enrolled in, and certainly in your professional life, you need to become aware of these media and their use in presentations.

A few general guidelines for proper selection and use of audio-visual media should be followed. When using an off-the-shelf film or tape carefully preview it to determine which portions are appropriate for your message. If the tape or film bores you, be kind to your audience and search elsewhere for material. When editing a film or tape take notes and prepare a brief handout for participants on salient points. Don't be afraid to stop and start the film or tape to provide immediate discussion. Answer questions and interpret the material's significance to your message.

VCR equipment

This equipment is available in most organizations or can be rented for a nominal fee. Earlier, I suggested a presentation addressing the topic of stopping smoking. An edited tape of prior smokers who have physical ailments, and are forced to carry oxygen tanks, or who present a negative image from having smoked, provides effective testimony for the speaker's message. Recall also the city council meeting where the citizen speaker recommends that the city streets require repair to avoid accidents and reduce repairs on automobiles. A video tape of motorists avoiding a pothole, screeching to a stop to avoid another motorist who has swerved to avoid the pothole and the back end of a car's motion, clearly documents the need for action by Council. The retirement ceremony cited earlier would be enhanced with a tape of the honoree which provides an edited version of a typical day in that person's life. Each of these examples represent instances where an audio-visual tape can be prepared in advance to illustrate or explain information, evoke emotion or feelings in the audience, and create or enhance a mood or climate.

With the availability of quality portable recording equipment only minimal skills are required to creatively design video tapes for diverse topics. VCR video display equipment is available in multiple sizes to accommodate large audiences. The equipment can also be used in a presentation to create immediate information for analysis. Consider for illustration the manager of bank tellers who wants to train personnel to present a "personal banker" approach to customers. The manager has organized a presentation which describes the skills desired and the behaviors which must be corrected. The manager may have used a previously edited tape of employee-customer interactions which illustrate positive and negative skills and behaviors. As part of the total presentation, the manager asks employees to form dyads and role play an interaction between a customer and teller in order to practice behaviors and skills. Taping of these role-playing situations followed by immediate replay and feedback is an effective presentational design to accomplish the manager's purpose. Use of the VCR as part of a presentation will not fit all topics, audiences, or occasions. The technique is powerful in providing information in a realistic manner.

The presenter in using a prepared tape needs to know how to operate the replay machine. The video screen should be placed for optimal viewing by the audience and the sound adjusted to the appropriate level. The presenter should join the audience or stand to the side to focus attention on the display. The information may be stopped at any point to provide immediate interpretation or to add emphasis to a future sequence of the tape. If you are using the equipment for taping the audience as in the earlier role-playing situation of bank teller and customer, allow the participants to critique or interpret their behaviors prior to your feedback. The presenter utilizing the VCR must learn new skills to create tapes and to effectively present the information.

Films

Films or segments of films are effective to present supporting information in a presentation. The availability of films has increased from multiple sources: film companies, university or college media centers, school districts, organizations, service agencies or local libraries. A film should be previewed to determine if it portrays both the information and the mood or climate desired for the presentation. A film can effectively portray motion, a process or operation, as well as emotions of the actors. The presenter may select only a segment of a film to portray an explicit situation which supports the theme of the speech.

When utilizing films, the presenter should normally provide a preface to its use. This may be as brief as "Please, attend to this segment of the film entitled 'Peege'".

The presenter may wish to spend more time in analysis and interpretation following viewing than setting the scene. Those decisions must be consistent with the overall plan for the presentation.

The skill in operation of projection equipment must be mastered by the presenter. Usually the visual quality is enhanced by dimming the lights. Thus, the presenter may need assistance from a member of the audience. The film should be prethreaded and ready for viewing only requiring the adjustment of sound for the audience. The film should be rewound after the presentation to minimize distraction of the audience. The presenter should move to the front of the room away from the projecting machine for interpretation. The projecting machine should either be moved or the audience seating arranged in advance so that contact with all audience members may be maintained. Films are effective support material for a presentation only if the subject of the film is pertinent, the film and acting is of high quality, the presenter is skilled in operation of the machine, and the presenter is skillful in introducing and interpreting the information.

Multi-Media Equipment

Multi-media involve the combination of several media. The VCR and film combine the use of auditory and visual signals into one vehicle or display. Speakers using 35 mm slides will often use several projectors simultaneously interfaced with background music or taped dialogue from a tape recorder. These are effective means of portraying information. Several excellent programs for service clubs and briefings for decision making groups have consisted of an introduction of the multi-media production, the production, following by a question and answer segment. The presenter's role is much different in this type of design than in a presentation where the speaker is the key person in imparting information.

Multi-media are effective for a presentation when multiple forms of media are needed to present information. The speaker sequences the use of a variety of audio-visuals to impart information and create a mood or climate. The pattern of the audio-visuals may consist of sequencing of charts on poster board, use of the chalkboard, a transparency of pertinent information followed by a film clip or segment of a film. The design or pattern which is used should consider the resources available, the time required, the space for the presentation, the skill level of the speaker in both equipment operation and interpretation skills, and the acceptability and utility of the medium for the audience.

Summary

The media of audio-visual include visual, audio, and audio-visual. Visuals include charts, maps, graphs, pictures, handouts, exhibits, models and objects or specimens. Visual display equipment includes chart boards, chalkboard, transparency/overhead projectors, slide projectors, filmstrip projectors, opaque projectors, and computer assisted graphics. Audio projection equipment includes a sound system, tape recorder and record player. Audio-visual equipment includes the VCR and film projector. Audio-visuals are effective means of depicting information but must be created and selected in a design which focuses on the reasons for speaking to a specific group on a specific topic. Audio-visuals are designed to support the presentation, not be the presentation.

Chapter Five

Audience Involvement: Questions Please

By

Robert Ross

Involvement of the audience in the speaking encounter can help both you and your audience accomplish your objectives. This chapter will address the speaker's role in encouraging and controlling audience involvement and in effectively responding to their questions and comments.

The speaker needs to consider several variables before deciding how to get the audience involved. Some of these variables include the degree of formality of the situation, the expectations of those individuals who may be in charge, the expectations of the group being addressed, and the style of the speaker.

First, let's consider occasions where the response is dictated or influenced by certain individuals. For example, an employee of an organization is frequently asked to provide a status report on a project and present the report to a small number of decision makers. The report is a speech which should follow the elements of composition and delivery described elsewhere in this textbook.

The supervisor or chair of the group, because of his or her position, may exercise some power and dictate that the speaker follow a particular procedure. While I was a high school teacher, I had two different principals. The first principal allowed me to set the rules for audience response. When I gave a report to her, I was allowed to present the report followed by a question and answer session. The other principal dictated a different approach which allowed the group to interrupt the report to ask immediate questions.

When I chaired Graduate Council one of my responsibilities was
to state the "ground rules" for an individual's request of, or
report to, the council. Included in these ground rules was an
explanation of the procedures I would follow in responding to
audience questions. The report was to be presented orally, followed
by questions by council members, followed by questions from audience
members (if present), followed by additional questions from council
members, and finally a summation by the speaker. The protocol
called for council members to formally address the presenter by Mr.,
Ms., or Doctor, followed by the question. The situation was
considered formal and the procedures or ground rules were dictated
by the chair based upon the customs followed by the group for the
event.

The first example illustrates a more informal situation with
the persons in control stating expectations for the question-answer
format. The second example illustrates a formal situation with
specific guidelines given to the speaker.

These examples illustrate the importance of how informal or
formal the situation is, the expectations of persons in power and
the group's expectations. In a classroom context these factors are
also important. Granted, there may be less power associated with
peers since they don't usually grade your presentation. However,
any student following a speaker who was especially skillful
recognizes that the standard for expected behavior has been raised.

The degree of formality for a classroom presentation will be
influenced by the expectations of the professor. The nature of the
topic, the mood created by the speaker, the speaker's communicative
style and the degree of familiarity with peers will also influence
this dimension. An informal and personal style of communicating is
normally expected and effective.

Competent speakers assess the expectations of their audience
and the individual who is in charge of the session, then consider
the degree of formality needed to accomplish their purposes. Once
these variables are known the speaker needs to announce the "rules"
that will guide audience involvement. The options for question and
answer rules include whether you will respond to questions at any
time, respond to questions at designated points, or respond to
questions only after conclusion of the speech.

The announcement should be included in the introduction of the
presentation so the audience is aware of the expected protocol. The
first option is not recommended for beginning speakers because
multiple interruptions may change the mood the speaker is trying to
create. The second option is effective for topics that are complex

and have natural division points where a brief question and answer session would allow the audience to clarify a particular point before the speaker moves on to a subsequent point in his or her speech. For speeches that are less than ten minutes in length the final option is preferred for the sake of convenience.

Therefore, the speaker should identify the audience's expectations, consider his/her own preferred style, determine when questions shall be allowed, and recognize the time limitations for the presentation prior to making a decision on the rules for the question and answer session. The remaining task is to announce to the audience in the introduction to the speech the procedure that will be used.

COMPONENTS OF THE QUESTION AND ANSWER SESSION

The components for an effective question and response session include the initiation of questioning, the six step process for each question or comment, closure of questioning, and closure of the presentation.

Initiation of the Question and Answer Session

The question and response component of a presentation begins with a clear statement by the speaker that questions are expected on the topic. If you have announced in the introduction to the speech that a question and response segment will follow your prepared material, a simple statement, "I am now open for questions," is all that is necessary. If you have not indicated in your introduction that a question and response segment will follow, a more focused statement may be necessary. For example, you might state, "Are there questions on the advantages and disadvantages of using seatbelts?" You are clearly stating a ground rule that comments are not questions, and that issues raised by audience members should focus on the topic of the speech.

If you wish to state or restate the rules you will follow during the question-answer response segment, you may do so at this time. For example, you might state, "I have six minutes for questions prior to closing. I will attempt to respond to each questioner by limiting individuals to one question until all of you have had an opportunity to react. I am available after the session for more discussion. [pause] I am now ready for the first question."

There should be a definite pause between the speech's conclusion prior to initiation of the statement that you are now prepared for questions. You may consider a purposeful movement toward the audience, stopping in front of them and stating "I am open for questions." Glancing around at individuals indicates that you have shifted to a transactional mode. This action also provides time for the audience to shift from being listeners to being active participants. The major task in initiating questions is to clearly separate the two segments of the presentations.

Six Step Process for the Question and Answer Session

The speaker's style of interacting with audience members depends on the degree of cooperation the audience members extend to the speaker. A particularly hostile or argumentative audience member should be addressed much differently than the audience member who asks a "neutral" question. The next section addresses many instances where variation of the six step process should occur. The purpose of this section, however, is to identify the usual pattern a speaker should follow in an interchange with an individual audience member.

Audience members may choose to make comments even though the "ground rules" stated that questions are expected. The speaker must respond to the audience member's utterance whether it be a question or a comment. The six step process is a model with guidelines for appropriate communication behavior. The six-step process is described in Figure 1:

Figure 1

Steps for Responding to Audience Questions

1. Active Listening   Appropriate nonverbal behaviors indicating that you are paying attention to the individual's utterance.

2. Clarification   A one-to-one exchange between you and the questioner to ensure you understand the intended meaning of the utterance.

3. Restatement   Repeat the question to the entire audience.

4. One-line Response   Answer the question in one simple sentence.

5.   Explanation   Extended   comments   which   link   the
                                 one-line response to the thesis of the
                                 speech.

6.   Follow-up   Ask the audience member whether the
                                 response   and   explanation   adequately
                                 answered the question.

Active Listening

     Active listening begins when you select the first questioner.
You should move closer to the questioner to carry on a more
conversational dialogue, but not so close that he or she is
uncomfortable. Remember, since you are standing and the questioner
is seated, it will be uncomfortable for both of you if you hover
over him or her. With a hostile or unfriendly question, hold your
ground and don't move backward. Further, you may want the rest of
the audience members to hear the exchange that will take place.
Individuals who are too close tend to lower their voices. Also,
provide direct eye contact during this step. Facial expressions
should indicate interest, attentiveness and involvement. Overall,
your behavior should be poised and attentive.

Clarifying the Question

     The negotiation of meaning of an audience member's utterance
involves employing appropriate nonverbal and oral skills. The
purpose of this step is to make sure you understand the question or
comment. We are all guilty of misinterpreting what others say so it
conforms to what we want to hear. You should continue the
interchange until the audience member is satisfied you understand
the comment and hopefully the question that was raised. One
approach is to paraphrase the audience member's utterance in your
own words. When you repeat their words you are "parrot-phrasing,"
rather than paraphrasing, and the intended meaning has not been
negotiated. Individual audience members may make a comment instead
of a question, may make an utterance which is confusing, may state
multiple questions in the same utterance or state a question which
has multiple meanings. Consider the following example of an
utterance that has multiple meanings:

Questioner: "How much money do you make each year?"

Speaker: "Are you interested in my personal salary
                         or the company profits?"

Questioner's: "The company's gross and net."

The active listening and negotiation of meaning steps are
interdependent and need to continue until you understand the
audience member's meaning.

    When the audience member's statement is very clear you can drop
the negotiation of meaning step. But, often this is not the case.
For example, "What time will we take a break?" may be interpreted as
"When do we take a short break for use of the restroom, to smoke or
have a cup of coffee or soft drink." You could ignore the
negotiation of meaning and respond with a statement, "Tom wants to
know when we take a break. That will be in twenty minutes." Tom
may follow-up with a statement, "No, I want to know when we break
for lunch." This misunderstanding could have been avoided, had you
attempted to find out if your interpretation of Tom's question was
correct.   When in doubt, quickly proceed through the negotiation
of meaning step prior to restatement.

Restate the Question

    When you restate the question for the audience, your verbal and
nonverbal behaviors should signify that you have shifted from an
interpersonal to a public speaking mode of communication. Prior to
your restatement you could move to a more central location in the
room, then while looking at the entire audience, restate the
question using more expansive gestures and volume that is loud
enough to be heard by everyone in the room.

    The reason for restatement is two-fold. First, not all members
of the audience can hear the conversation between the questioner and
speaker. Second, the restatement allows the speaker to focus the
question while retaining the intent of the questioner. In the
following example, restatement is used to defuse a hostile question.

Question: "How can you justify the use of U.S. funds
                         to support murderers in Nicaragua who
                         wander the countryside butchering and
                         slaughtering innocent women and children?"

Restate: "Jane would like to know how continued aid
                            is justified in terms of recent reports of
                            human rights violation."

When you restate a question, you must be careful to preserve
the intent of the questioner. When clarifying the meaning of the
question, you should have asked, "Are you concerned with reports of
human rights violations?." If you receive a positive reply, then
when you use the phrase in restatement you are likely to be
perceived by the audience members who heard the exchange as being
fair in interpreting the questioners meaning.

The use of restatement may be eliminated under certain
circumstances. When you are in a small room and everybody hears the
question or in a larger room and the questioner speaks loudly or
uses a microphone, restatement might not be necessary.

One-Line Response

The one-line response should be a thesis statement. After
hearing the question, the audience receives a simple clear response.
The exception to starting with a one-line response is when you need
to state certain qualifications prior to responding. These
occasions are rare but when they occur, the speaker needs only to
follow the restatement with a brief remark before answering the
question. For example, state to the audience, "Before I answer this
question I'd like to state a couple of points which will clarify my
response." Clearly and directly state the qualifiers followed by a
one-line response and then an explanation.

Explanation

Explanation is an opportunity to provide additional support for
your answer. In some instances the explanation may be lengthy (i.e.
one to two minutes) but the norm for most questions is fifteen to
thirty seconds. When the one-line response is very clear, an
explanation may not be needed. For example, "What evidence did you
have for your point on . . .?" Following restatement the speaker
might state in a one-line response, "I utilized an article by
Kissinger in Foreign Affairs Quarterly. Does that answer your
question?"

Explanation is an excellent opportunity to clarify your thesis,
but for some questions or comments it would be redundant or
detrimental. For instance, if someone asks "What is the time?"
answer the question--don't explain how to make a watch.

Follow-Up

     The final step is to follow-up with the questioner to determine
if your response answered the question or comment. When you follow
up, you should recognize that you are shifting to an interpersonal
style of communicating. You should move closer to the audience
member who asked the question, look him or her directly in the eye
and state in a clear but lower tone of voice, "Did I answer your
question?" If the response is yes, proceed to the next question.
If the answer is no, you are back to active listening and
negotiation of meaning.

     There are instances where the use of a follow-up is not
advisable. When the questioner is especially argumentative or is
attempting to dominate the question-answer time, don't follow-up.
Other instances are mentioned in the planning for and implementing
speaker-audience interchanges section of this chapter.

     Although the six steps I've described provide a useful set of
guidelines for responding to audience questions or comments, things
may happen during a particular session that can make some deviation
necessary. The speaker must make decisions during each interchange
regarding which steps are needed.

     The evaluation criteria, which are presented later in this
book, include a tabulation form for each audience-speaker exchange.
The evaluation criteria are adjusted based upon appropriate
decision-making and effective implementation of your decision.

     When the time allowed for questions expires, the remaining two
tasks are closure of the question-response segment and closure of
the presentation.

Closure of the Question and Answer Session

     The speaker should be cognizant of both the time allowed for
the interchange and the interest level of the audience. Some
organizations have specific time limits which must be adhered to in
order to complete the agenda and be fair to other speakers. When
you know there is only time for one more question, announce that
fact to the audience by saying, "I have time for one more question."

     When the audience still seems interested in asking questions
after your time is up, a clear statement to acknowledge that
interest might be, "I appreciated your questions , but I am afraid
our time is up. I notice that there are several additional

questions.   I am available after class in case you'd like to talk
further."

On the other hand, when there are no further questions, you can
say, "I see there are no further questions. Thank you for your
involvement."

Effectively closing the question and answer session allows the
speaker to retain control of the situation and helps to build his or
her credibility. Closure of the question and answer session should
be followed by closure of the presentation.

Closure of the Presentation

The question and answer session is not the final component of
your presentation. A final conclusion allows you to focus the
listener's thoughts. The final summation may be as short as twenty
seconds or as long as a minute. A transition to the conclusion
should be included in your closure of the question and answer
session. For example, "I see there are no further questions. Thank
you for showing an interest in the issue of requiring a second
language as part of the high school curriculum. Please allow me to
leave you with some thoughts on the subject . . ."

You might want to pause for three to five seconds while moving
to a central location before your conclusion. The conclusion to the
presentation is an opportunity to provide closure. A well-planned
and delivered conclusion sets the mood for the speech and gives you
an opportunity to reassert the central idea of your speech.

PLANNING AND IMPLEMENTING THE QUESTION AND ANSWER SESSION

The importance of planning for the question and answer session
is discussed in this section. The first topic deals with the
speaker's credibility. And the second area addresses audience
reaction in the form of comments and questions. Finally,
encouraging audience participation in the question and answer
session is discussed.

Retaining Credibility

The competent speaker should spend as much time preparing for
the question and answer session as for the speech. Your credibility
as a speaker is on the line during this part of your presentation.

A speaker retains credibility in several ways, but a few considerations in responding to questions include the following:

Don't Bluff or "Stone-Wall"

When you don't have an appropriate response or don't know the answer, simply say so, and proceed to the next question. Consider the following example:

Question: "How does Colorado compare to Kansas in funding for higher education?"

Response: "I don't know the answer to your question, but I have some information with me and we can look it up after the presentation. Would you mind meeting me after the presentation to get this information?"

Question: "What was the state subsidy for attracting high technology industry in 1985?"

Response: "I don't have those specific figures, but they are available from the Governor's Office. As you recall, my thesis focused on all forms of industry and that figure was $40,000. Are there other questions?"

A rambling response which does not answer the question, a "no comment" or a Nixon ploy of "stone-walling" the questioner by shifting to the next questioner will not work. The competent speaker attempts to relate the question to facts he or she knows as in the second example. Minimally, the speaker presents a confident, personal style, responding to the question and the questioner in a concise fashion. Don't BLUFF or RAMBLE or your credibility will be lost.

Use Effective Nonverbal Behaviors

Moving purposefully to the questioner, using direct eye contact with the questioner while clarifying the question, using direct eye contact with the audience when responding, using vocal variety to express your feelings and projecting so you can be heard, will communicate poise and self-assurance.

Express Honest Feelings

Many times an audience member will attempt to bait the speaker, become argumentative, or in general, will be hostile toward you or the topic. The first thing to remember is that you are in control. Not all audience members are hostile, only one individual. In fact, most members of your audience are probably angry at the questioner for acting in an obnoxious manner. Second, the anger or hostility is probably directed toward the topic and not you. The following examples illustrate approaches to two possible scenarios:

Topic:	"Abortion Should Be Legal"
Questioner:	(Baiting) "Would you kill your own child?!"
Response:	"Your question causes me pain; however, it is a fair question. Yes, if I were raped and decided it was best, I would have an abortion."
Topic:	"Abortion Should Be the Legal"
Questioner:	(Antagonistic/preaching) "You mean you would kill innocent babies when you know it is against God's laws?"
Response:	"You are raising issues about God's laws which are open to interpretation by each individual. Your loaded question indicates you have a definite opinion. I respect your opinion and ask that you respect mine.

The speaker needs to remain calm and in control. You can attempt to diffuse the person's hostility by responding to his or her question. If the questioner isn't satisfied and continues to talk, the best approach is to let them know they are out of line.

Respond Directly To the Intent Of the Question

When clarifying a question, you should determine what the questioner is asking. After a simple restatement, answer the question as directly and concisely as possible.

Your credibility can be enhanced or maintained by not bluffing a response, using effective nonverbal behaviors, expressing honest feelings and responding directly to the question. In addition, if you don't prepare for audience questions, there is a good chance you'll be "caught off guard" which would damage your overall credibility.

Preparing for Comments and Questions: Audience's response

Audience responses to a speech are of two forms: questions and comments. Questions generally ask for the speaker to clarify a point, answer a concern or provide additional support for a major point. A comment is a statement by the audience member in which an opinion is expressed. In this section we deal with some special problems involving comments and questions.

Comments as a Form of Response

The first form of audience response we will examine is a comment. Comments my be neutral, supportive or opposing. Several examples show how you can interpret the comment as a question and thus respond further.

The first example we will examine is a comment which is supportive of the speech's main thesis. This is followed by responses of three hypothetical speakers:

Topic: Crime Must be Controlled by Harsher Penalties

Audience Member: "I didn't realize that crime had increased that much". [Nonverbals indicate that the individual agrees with the evidence presented.]

Speaker One: "Yes, crime has risen. Thank you for recognizing the seriousness of the issue. Are there other questions?"

Speaker Two: Yes, crime has risen. Do you have a question?"

Speaker Three: "Do you have a question instead of a comment?"

Let's look briefly at these different responses. Speaker three uses only the first two steps of the process: active listening and clarification. The bluntness of the response is rather impersonal and does not acknowledge the supportiveness of the audience member's comment.

The second response is still focused primarily on the first two steps of active listening and clarification. The difference is that the speaker clearly acknowledges the questioner's content in the statement "Yes, crime has risen." This would satisfy steps three and four: restatement and one-line response. When the speaker responds with "Do you have a question?" he or she moves the process back to step two—clarification. Speaker one responds effectively to the comment by thanking the individual for the supportive remark, then asking for a question.

Audience members may also state a comment which opposes your position. Consider the following example from the audience member who makes a valid point opposing to your thesis.

Audience Member: "Air bags are only good for head-on collisions and not for side collisions."

Speaker: "John raised the question of the utility of air bags for side collisions. Your point is appropriate. It's true that air bags are not helpful in the side collision. However, the use of air bags is still viable because we want to protect as many folks as possible. Only 10 percent of accidents are side collisions. Air bags will address the other 90 percent."

The speaker must acknowledge the validity of the argument before explaining why the single exception does not invalidate the thesis. The use of follow-up may be omitted when addressing a comment which is contrary to your thesis.

Comments by an audience member which are extremely hostile or argumentative call for a different response. Consider the following example for analysis:

Topic: Capital Punishment Must Lead to the Death Penalty.

Audience: "What a bunch of hogwash!"

Speaker One: "You seem to be upset by the topic. I am willing to listen to your opinion after the presentation to understand how we differ. (pause) Are there other questions?"

Speaker Two: "I'm not clear on what your question is, but I can see you are personally involved in the

topic. Since your opinion will take some
time to understand, I would appreciate
discussing the topic with you after the
presentation. Are there other questions?"

Both speakers acknowledge the audience member's intense feeling
on the topic, but tactfully postpone a discussion until after the
presentation.

Often, the audience members who are very emotional, have not
developed their thinking to the point where they are prepared to ask
a question. The purpose of a question and answer session is to
address the entire audience, not devote your time to a single
respondent.

Comments should be expected during a question-answer session.
You should prepare for the different types of comments on your major
points. Now, let's shift our attention to the audience's use of
questions.

Questions as a Form of Response

While the reasons for asking questions vary, generally, they
request clarification of a point for additional evidence to support
your thesis, or a response to a concern they have about the topic.
The questions may be neutral, opposing or supportive of your
thesis. All three categories may be affected by the audience
member's intentional use of multiple, confusing, or leading
questions.

Multiple Questions

Sometimes, a speaker asks more than a single question. This is
referred to as a multiple question.

Topic: Higher Education Deserves Adequate Funding

Questioner: "Where did you get the data to support your claim?
            But will more money really solve the problem? ...ah
            ...um ...Doesn't Gramm-Rudman complicate the
            situation . . ."

Speaker: "You have asked three different questions in your
            response! You have been listening actively!
            [Complimentary Humor] Let me start by responding

to 'Where did I get my data?'. [Repeat] The data
as you recall was from . . . Another question you
raised was, 'Will Gramm-Rudman complicate funding
of Higher Education?' [Repeat] Yes, it will impact
directly on adequate funding. (one-liner) The
impact to Colorado according to State Senator Bond
is . . . (explanation) That leaves us with your
final question, 'Will money solve the problem?'
(repeat) Yes, money is the key to trigger an
affordable quality education. (one-liner) The
state of New York spends . . . (explanation) Thank
you Juan for your insightful questions. Are there
other questions?"

The speaker has the option to ask the audience member which
single question he or she wishes to have answered based upon ground
rules that permit one question at a time for each audience member.
The speaker can also ask which question the audience member wishes
answered first (clarification of the question).

Confused Question

Sometimes the audience member is confused and needs the
assistance of the speaker to focus the question. Consider the
following example:

Topic: Higher Education Deserves Adequate Funding

Questioner: "Well, resources seem to be a problem ...ah ...I
mean, the issue is adequate money ... How will
students pay more? ...ah ...What a mess . . ."

Speaker: "Yes, adequate funding of higher education is a
mess. Are you asking for clarity on the role of
students in addressing this problem?"

The speaker must assist the questioner in selecting the
question which reflects the questioners thinking. However, the
speaker may utilize the opportunity to reinforce the main point of
the speech.

Leading Questions

The use of a leading question by the audience member can also
occur. Leading questions suggest a desired response; they put

pressure on the respondent to answer in a certain way. Consider the following examples of supportive and opposing leading questions:

Topic: The English Essay Exam Should Be Discontinued.

Question: "My friends in the dorm feel that the English Essay Exam is positive, what do you think?"

Speaker: "The question asked is 'Do I think the English Essay Exam is positive?' [repeat] I recognize that some students and faculty support the current English Essay Exam. But no, it is not positive in its current form and should be eliminated. [one-line response] As you recall, . . ."

The questioner has asked a leading question which puts pressure on you to arrive at a position contrary to your main idea. The speaker effectively responded by acknowledging the opposite position and then stating his/her own opinion followed by an explanation. The speaker should then move to another questioner.

Leading questions can also be supportive of the speaker's thesis. Consider the following example for illustration:

Topic: COPIRG Funding Should be Increased

Questioner: "According to the school newspaper, COPIRG conducted the research for renter's rights and legal assistance for students. Do you believe those projects assist students?"

Speaker: "Susan asked if renters rights and legal assistance for students are other examples of projects sponsored by COPIRG which helped students? [repeat] Yes, they have assisted students and, with increased funding, the other projects I have mentioned could be accomplished. [one-line response and explanation] Thank you for identifying additional Copirg projects which protect students. Are there other questions?"

The leading question by the audience member indicated support for COPIRG but not necessarily for increased funding. The speaker needs to discuss other projects that COPIRG has effectively accomplished and link that evidence to the major thesis of the speech--increase in funding. The speaker can follow-up with the questioner directly or shift to the next question. My preference is to shift to the next audience member.

All questions and comments by audience members may be leading or expressed in a confusing or multiple utterance form. The competent speaker develops their skill in responding appropriately to these types of questions and comments.

ENCOURAGING AUDIENCE PARTICIPATION

The major focus developed in this section is the encouragement of audience questions. Audience participation will be influenced by the speaker's nonverbal behavior, the audience's nonverbal behavior, or the speaker's previous response to a question.

The speaker's nonverbal behaviors indicate receptiveness to audience participation. A speaker who states "Are there questions?" in a harsh or hesitant voice may indicate to the audience "I dare you to ask a question!" or "Have pity on me. Please don't challenge me." A speaker's eye contact with the audience may indicate he or she is ready for questions, whereas, a downward cast of the eyes may send a message, "I asked for involvement; but I will not recognize you." Similarly, where you stand in the room indicates whether you are interested in questions. A movement from the podium or from behind a desk, closer to the audience indicates that you are interested in answering questions.

In addition, your facial expressions should show that you are genuinely interested in the reactions of the audience. If you look bitter or cocky, they will not be encouraged to ask many questions.

The audience's nonverbal behaviors are equally important during the exchange. Each time you ask "Are there questions?" you should make a "mental note" of those persons who raised their hands. When you are ready to proceed to another question you can then refer immediately to one of the individuals who raised his or her hand moments ago. If allowed, obnoxious audience members are likely to ask a new question in an attempt to dominate the question and answer session.

The speaker's manner of responding to previous questions and comments from audience members will also influence future and potential questioners. When responding, the speaker should consider the following guidelines:

- A response indicates respect for the questioner.
- A restatement of the question or comment preserves the intent of the utterance.
- The response should be relevant to the question or comment.

The Problem of the Hostile Audience Member

In most cases a speaker is concerned with ensuring that the audience participates actively in the question and answer session. In a few cases, the speaker must be concerned with a related yet very different problem.

Occasionally, a speaker will be faced with an unusually hostile or argumentative individual. The argumentative audience member may start with an opposing question or statement. After your response the questioner may not respect your nonverbal shift to another audience member. This person wants to continue the "fight." Some individuals have even interrupted the speaker while they have been responding to the hostile member's question to raise additional questions.

Your response needs to indicate you are in control and that you do not appreciate their hostile behavior. You can attempt to offer a "face-saving" comment to allow you both to shift to a more reasonable communicative style. A possible response might be as follows:

Response: "You certainly seem to be involved in the topic. I also am concerned. It appears you have several issues that require a response. Since the time allotted for questions and answers is brief, let's meet later to discuss the topic. Are there other questions?"

The importance of control by the speaker in this situation needs to be stressed. If the hostile audience member continues, your response needs to be more blunt. Incorporating humor or social norms into a second response sometimes will work to lower the individual's intensity level or force them to accept a more reasonable strategy because of other audience members social pressure.

CONCLUSION

This chapter focused on answering audience questions. The importance of analyzing the situation and the audience was

identified in the establishment of "ground rules" for the question
and answer session. The four components of this part of a
presentation included initiation of the questioning segment, the six
steps for addressing a specific question or comment from an
individual audience member, closure of the question and answer
segment and finally closure of the presentation. The difference
between comments and questions as forms of audience response was
clarified. Strategies for speaker response to neutral, supporting
and opposing audience remarks and questions were developed through
use of examples. Finally, a method of encouraging audience
participation was discussed.

Chapter Six

Delivery

By

Martin Remland

If I asked you to name a politician or a celebrity you considered to be a good speaker, who would you name? What is it about the person that makes him or a her good speaker? Now, using your own personal criteria, how would you rank order the following personalities as public speakers?

_____Geraldine Ferraro   _____Jesse Jackson
_____Johnny Carson   _____Barbara Walters
_____Dan Rather   _____Jimmy Carter
_____Katherine Hepburn   _____Ronald Reagan
_____Howard Cosell   _____Joan Rivers

In your efforts to rank order these speakers perhaps you found yourself thinking about how they sound or what they do while speaking rather than what they say. For example, you might have thought about the slow and measured pace that Ronald Reagan uses, the explosive movements that characterize a Joan Rivers monologue, the southern accent and monotone voice of Jimmy Carter, or the nasal diatribes of Howard Cosell. If so, you already have determined for yourself what this chapter is about. The vocal and physical expressions of a speaker (i.e., enunciation, volume, intonation, facial expression, gestures, posture) represent what those of us in the field of human communication call delivery or nonverbal communication.

Broadly speaking, delivery includes everything you hear a speaker say and see a speaker do, except for the words that are spoken. Try to imagine yourself listening to a speaker from another country talking in a language you don't understand. Is that speaker communicating to you? Researchers have determined that a great deal of information is indeed conveyed through nonverbal actions. In fact, one well known social psychologist has estimated that as much as 93% of our interpretation is of a speaker's facial expressions and vocal inflection (Mehrabian, 1972). Thus, when forming an opinion of how a speaker feels about a subject, listeners don't pay much attention to words when other channels of communication are readily available.

In addition to attitudes and feelings, a speaker's delivery also leads to an array of inferences on the part of listeners, ranging from how intelligent they feel a speaker is to the kind of personality they think the speaker has. For example, a speaker who is able to maintain eye contact with his or her audience will tend to be judged as more knowledgeable by audience members than a speaker who is unable to maintain eye contact. And researchers have found that similar sorts of impressions result from a speaker's rate of speech, body shape, vocal quality, attire, posture, etc. In recent years, this kind of "body language" literature has prompted more than a few hucksters to try and sell the notion that people can be manipulated rather easily with a flick of the wrist, a flirtatious glance, or a provocative lean. Rarely is this the case however, given the complex nature of impression formation processes. Nor is it true, as many body language gurus once espoused, that you can read a person like a book. With few exceptions, (i.e. facial expressions and certain kinds of symbolic gestures) the idea that every movement has a discrete meaning is absurd. The best way to read a person like a book is to get their memoirs.

In this chapter I'll explore the general subject of speech delivery in three major sections. In the first section, I introduce the terminology needed to understand the components of delivery. Then, in the following section I discuss the primary dimensions of good delivery. Finally, in the last section I consider some of the methods available for improving the delivery of a speech.

THE BASIC ELEMENTS OF DELIVERY

Naturally, before we consider the characteristics of good delivery we need to identify the key concepts and processes that comprise delivery. The best way to do this is to first discuss what delivery consists of and then to discuss how the delivery (nonverbal communication) of a speech relates to the content (verbal communication) of the speech.

What Does Delivery Consist Of?

Most textbooks on public speaking divide the subject of delivery into two main categories: the auditory elements of delivery (what listeners hear) and the visual elements of delivery (what listeners see). I can't think of a better way to approach the subject.

The Auditory Elements of Delivery

In large part, delivery consists of the vocal characteristics of speech; those things we would hear exclusively if the words of a speaker were unintelligible. However, before discussing each of these auditory elements, let's begin with a brief account of the speech production process in order to gain some understanding of how humans speak.

The process of speech production involves inhalation, exhalation, phonation, resonation, and articulation. A brief description follows:

INHALATION--Entering our nose or mouth, the air we breathe in passes down our pharynx (throat), larynx (the "voice box" where our vocal cords are located), trachea (a tube in our neck commonly known as the windpipe), bronchial tubes (located in our chest cavity), and into our lungs.

EXHALATION--By relaxing our diaphragm (a large "dome shaped" muscle that separates our chest cavity from our abdominal cavity), and contracting the muscles of our chest and abdomen, we force air up from our lungs.

PHONATION--Traveling through our bronchial tubes, trachea, and pharynx, the exhaled air enters our larynx passing through a small regulated opening between our vocal cords called the glottis. When our vocal cords are tightened with muscular tension, they vibrate as the air goes through. The vibration of our vocal cords produces a sound like the vibrations of a violin string. This process determines the "pitch" of our voice, or how high or low it sounds.

RESONATION--The sound produced by our vibrating vocal cords is amplified and modified as it travels through the cavities of our throat, mouth, and nose. This process determines the "quality" of our voice, or how distinctive it sounds.

ARTICULATION--The sound produced by the vibration of our vocal cords and resonated by our throat, mouth, and nose chambers, is shaped by our articulators: tongue, lips, teeth, palate, and jaw. This process enables us to "enunciate" words skillfully and to "pronounce" them correctly.

Now we can focus more clearly on the six key elements that make up the auditory component of speech delivery. The six elements are: pitch, quality, volume, enunciation, pronunciation, and rate.

Pitch.

The pitch of our voice, as I noted above, is determined by the vibrations of our vocal cords. The more the vocal cords vibrate, the higher pitched the voice sounds. The number of times per second our vocal cords vibrate is referred to as the voice's fundamental frequency and is affected by how tense the vocal cords are, how long they are, and how thick they are. Generally, men have "deeper" voices than women do because they have longer and thicker vocal cords, which means fewer vibrations.

The pitch of our voice communicates how we feel. When we get angry or very excited, for example, the intensity of the emotion causes us to tighten our vocal cords which raises the pitch of our voice. The relaxed muscles associated with more passive emotions, such as contempt and sadness, result in a lower pitched voice.

Quality.

How would you describe the "sound" of your voice? While it's not too difficult to say that you have a high pitched or a low pitched voice, it's a lot harder to describe all of the other characteristics that make your voice unique. And that's what vocal quality or the "timbre" of your voice refers to. The distinctive quality of our voice depends on the size, shape, and texture of our resonators--the chambers of the throat, mouth, and nose. The sounds of voices differ in much the same way that the sounds of musical instruments differ. We shouldn't expect George to sound like Fred any more than we would expect a trumpet to sound like a french horn.

Volume.

Also called vocal intensity, the volume of our voice is how loud or soft the tone is. When we speak, we relax our diaphragm and contract the muscles of our abdomen and chest in order to expel air with a force sufficient to produce sound. The more forcefully we expel air, the louder our voice will sound.

Enunciation.

When we engage the services of our articulators--mainly the lips, tongue, and jaw--we are able to transform sound into words. The clarity with which we utter each word is referred to as enunciation or articulation. When Mary says, "the U.S. jus isn't doin enough to meet the needs of the homeless." it's obvious that the words "just" and "doing" are not being clearly articulated because she has developed a tendency to avoid the work needed to enunciate those words.

Pronunciation.

Whereas enunciation refers to how distinctly words are expressed, pronunciation is how correctly they are expressed. One way to think of the difference between enunciation and pronunciation is to think of the former as a matter of skill and the latter as a matter of knowledge. For example, Henry might say "git" instead of saying "get", not because he doesn't know how the word "get" is correctly pronounced but because it's easier to say "git" (you don't need to open your mouth as much saying "git" as you do saying "get"). Also, some people have trouble saying the word "statistics" and end up saying "stastistics" (adding the s) instead. The end result is not due to ignorance but a lack of skill in saying that particular word.

Speakers who do not pronounce a word correctly are not aware of how the word should be expressed. They may not know which syllable in the word to accent, whether a letter is supposed to be silent, or how a particular vowel should sound. For example, not knowing that the "b" in "subtle" is silent would cause someone to say, "you're not very sub-tl" instead of, "you're not very su-tl."

Rate.

The sixth and final audible element of speech delivery is how fast we talk, or the rate of our speech. Usually measured in words per minute, speech rate is a function of how quickly we can: a) generate the idea we want to express, b) select the words we want to use to express the idea, and c) move our lips, tongue and jaw in order to articulate the words. How fast does the average person speak? While no exact data are available, the typical estimate is close to 150 words per minute.

Even the most intelligent and articulate speaker can experience difficulty "encoding" his or her thoughts. This difficulty will show up in various kinds of pauses (also referred to as hesitations or dysfluencies). An unfilled pause is simply a silent gap between words. A filled pause is what we usually hear as "uh's" and "uhm's."

Of course, pauses often are used by speakers to create a dramatic effect or to stress an important point. Similarly, a speaker can choose to extend or drag "Heeeeerrrrre's Johnny."

To briefly review this section, the process of speech production consists of inhalation and exhalation. Phonation, which occurs in the voice box or larynx, produces the sound that is resonated in the cavities of the throat, mouth, and nose. Articulation involves the use of the lips, tongue, jaw, palate, and teeth to turn sounds into words. The six basic audible elements of human speech delivery are pitch, quality, volume, enunciation, pronunciation, and rate. In the next section, I'll introduce the basic nonverbal aspects of delivery that we see rather than hear.

The Visual Elements of Delivery

Imagine watching someone on television giving a lecture, speech, monologue, or sermon. Try to imagine what it would be like to turn the sound off. Doing so would allow you to focus on the speaker's facial expressions, posture, clothing, gestures, eye contact, and physical features. These are the variables that comprise the visual elements of a speaker's delivery. For convenience, I'll divide these elements into two categories: the physical movement of a speaker and the physical appearance of a speaker.

Physical Movement.

What are the different types of bodily and facial movements that we need to be concerned with? There are five basic types: emblems, adapters, illustrators, affect displays, and regulators. Each type of movement serves a different function and communicates a different kind of message. Let's begin by discussing emblems.

Emblems are movements that come the closest to being the gestural equivalents of words. Like words, there is a lot of agreement about what emblems mean in a given culture or in a particular profession. Can you communicate the following messages without using any words whatsoever?

> "I can't hear you, speak up"
> "How could I be so stupid"
> "She's over there"
> "Be quiet."
> "It looks OK to me"
> "What time do you have?"

Adaptors are movements that satisfy some physical or psychological need. Examples of adaptors include: crossing your legs, touching your nose, rubbing your arms, scratching your neck, bending your finger. Unlike emblems, they are not intended to communicate information and occur less often in social interactions than they do in private. Research on adaptors shows that they are associated with feelings of insecurity and anxiety. People touch themselves more and fiddle with objects more when they are uncomfortable than when they are relaxed.

Illustrators are a third type of movement. Illustrations are movements that visualize, emphasize, or merely accompany speech. When Gloria tries to explain to a friend how to serve in volleyball she might use her body to illustrate the proper stance, movement, etc. When Bob is asked how tall someone is he might reply by putting his hand next to his head to illustrate the approximate height of that person.

Illustrators also can emphasize what we say. In writing we can underline or capitalize certain words to make them stand out to our readers. In a speaking situation, we can jab, chop, extend an arm, or clench our fist to let our listeners know that an idea is especially important or to simply catch their attention. But in general, illustrators can include the expressive movements that occur naturally when we speak. Can you speak comfortably without moving your head or body?

Affect displays are movements that express our emotions. Generally, our facial expressions define the emotion we are experiencing. If someone is angry, you'll be able to see the anger in that person's face. Her lips might be pressed together, her eyes might seem to bug out, her brows will be lowered. These universal facial expressions of emotion include, in addition to anger: sadness, fear, disgust, joy, and surprise. And to complicate matters, the face is capable of expressing various combinations of these basic emotions at the same time.

Regulators are the final kind of movement that we need to briefly consider. These movements manage the turn-taking activity in speaking-listening interactions. A speaker uses regulators to send the following messages to his/her listeners:

> "I want to continue speaking so don't interrupt me"
> "I don't want to speak anymore so now you can speak"

And a listener uses regulators to send these messages to the speaker:

> "I'm interested in what you're saying so keep speaking"
> "I'd like to speak now"

These messages are communicated by eye contact, body lean, head nods, body tension, shoulder orientation, and other subtle movements. Of course, since regulators control turn-taking, they are significant in situations where the roles of speaker and listener shift back and forth a great deal; something that is not characteristic of a public speaking situation (unless time is allowed for a discussion or question and answer session).

On the other hand, to illustrate the importance of regulators, consider the case of Paul. When he maintains eye contact with an audience, faces them directly, moves close to them, etc., he conveys the message that he wants to continue in the role of speaker. These actions make it much easier for those in the audience to continue in the role of listeners than if Paul's behavior suggested his disinterest in speaking to them.

Physical Appearance.

Few would deny that a speaker's appearance can communicate to an audience. The clothes that Maria wears to class when she gives her speech, for example, can convey her: personality, socioeconomic status, age, nationality, values, attitude toward the course, knowledge of fashion, group affiliation, or even occupation. And Maria's physical features are likely to influence the audience's first impressions of her in somewhat predictable ways. Her height, weight, hair color, skin color, body shape, and general attractiveness will determine, to some extent, how positively or negatively she is perceived by her audience.

To conclude, the visual elements of speech delivery consist of those things we see rather than hear. A speaker's movement can include emblems, adaptors, illustrators, affect displays, and regulators. The physical appearance of a speaker includes those things that are relatively easy to manage, such as the clothes that are worn, and enduring qualities, such as height and skin color, that cannot be altered by the speaker.

How Does Delivery Relate to the Content of a Speech?

In the previous section I introduced the basic components of delivery; the various audible and visual factors that represent a speaker's nonverbal communication. Now, we need to consider how these delivery elements work with the content or verbal component of a speech. What impact will a speaker's delivery have on the message he or she is trying to get across?

A Speakerds Delivery Can Substitute for the Verbal Message

The principle here is not that a speaker doesn't need to say anything, but that often actions can adequately take the place of words. Sometimes a facial expression, a pause, an immediate gesture, or a head nod, can communicate faster and more effectively than words can. For example, when a speaker is asked an embarrassing or funny question, a smile might be a better response than saying, "that's an embarrassing question" or "I think that's very funny." Too, the use of emblems makes it unnecessary to say certain things because emblems are so readily understood. A "thumbs up" sign, for instance, is not likely to be misinterpreted.

A Speakerds Delivery Can Repeat the Verbal Message

Oral communication makes it possible to be redundant without necessarily being dull. Literally saying something twice likely will be more boring to an audience than saying something verbally and nonverbally at the same time. For example, holding up two fingers while saying, "the second reason I'm against this proposal is that it's too expensive," is an effective way to reinforce the fact that you're introducing a second point. Similarly, if you smile as you begin your speech while saying, "I'm happy to be here today," you've told your audience verbally and nonverbally that you're happy to be speaking to them. And when a speaker says, "I don't know," while holding up the palms of her hands and shrugging

her shoulders she has conveyed her message in two different channels
simultaneously.

A Speakerds Delivery Can Emphasize the Verbal Message

One of the most obvious and important ways that a speaker's
delivery can affect the content of his speech is by emphasizing
important ideas. When you say, "military aid should NOT be sent to
totalitarian regimes," stressing the word "not" by raising the tone
of your voice, you have used your delivery to indicate that you feel
strongly about this issue. In a similar way, pauses, variations in
pitch or rate, eye contact, and gestures, can effectively underline
the ideas of a speaker. In addition, a speaker can physically move
from one place to another to emphasize movement in her speech from
one point to another. For instance, while slowly walking to the
side, Kathy might say, "now that I've discussed the problem of air
pollution, let's consider some possible solutions."

A Speakerds Delivery Can Contradict the Verbal Message

How would you react to a speaker who, in a dull and lifeless
monotone voice, says, "I'm very excited to have this opportunity to
talk to you about a subject that is very important to me." Surely,
you would doubt the speaker's enthusiasm because of the sluggish way
in which her opening line was delivered. This illustrates one way
in which our nonverbal actions can contradict what we say. When
someone screams at the top of his lungs in an incredibly hostile
tone, "I'm not angry!" it's doubtful that he'll be believed.

But these kinds of contradictory messages often are expressed
deliberately in order to be sarcastic. Imagine, for example, a
speaker discussing the problem of poverty in the U.S. saying, with a
deadly serious expression and in a somber tone, "What's the quickest
way to eliminate poverty in this country? Get rid of all the poor
people." While the serious manner contradicts an obviously flippant
remark, few would take the speaker's remark seriously because of the
apparent sarcasm.

A Speakerds Delivery Can Complement the Verbal Message

Put simply, this means that the audible and visual elements of
a speaker's delivery provide an additional source of information.
While David's words tell us what his beliefs are on the subject of
abortion, his nonverbal actions tell us how strongly he feels about
the subject or whether he is uncomfortable talking about it.
Additionally, we are exposed to an assortment of cues which may be

indicative of David's personality, birthplace, relative age, physical health, etc. There is an axiom in the field of human communication which states unequivocally, "we cannot not communicate."

A Speakerds Delivery Can Regulate the Verbal Message

As I noted earlier in my discussion on movement, certain kinds of actions called regulators control the turn-taking that occurs between speaker and listener. In a discussion, where the roles of speaker and listener change frequently, a speaker can let her audience know that she wants to "hold the floor" by looking up to signal that she is thinking of what to say next or by maintaining tension in her face and posture. She can let her audience know that she is ready for another question by raising her eyebrows (this universal expression is called an "eyebrow flash" and is recognized instantly as an invitation to interact). On the other hand, a speaker can effectively assume the role of active listener encouraging audience members to speak by nodding her head, uttering sounds like "uh huh", maintaining eye contact, and adopting attentive postures and positions.

In this section I've explored some of the ways speech delivery interacts with speech content in a public speaking situation. Naturally, we can expect a speaker's delivery to emphasize, repeat, complement, or substitute for, some of his ideas. But a speaker's delivery also can contradict what is being said, and when not done purposefully, as in the special case of sarcasm, the inconsistency can create a bad impression. Finally, a speaker's delivery can control the content of speaker-audience exchanges by influencing turn-taking activity.

Up to this point, I've introduced the essentials of speech delivery without considering the things that a speaker can and should do to develop a good delivery. In the next major section of this chapter, I address this issue. The focus will be on identifying the characteristics of good delivery and on making recommendations designed to improve your delivery in the speeches you'll be assigned to give in this course.

THE BASIC DIMENSIONS OF GOOD DELIVERY

The overriding principle that will guide my analysis in this section is that a speaker's delivery is good when:

1. It is not distracting.
2. It is easily comprehended.
3. It suggests expertise on the topic.
4. It expresses interest in the topic.
5. It expresses interest in the audience.

This principle should seem fairly obvious. Can a speaker's delivery be good if you can't comprehend what the speaker is saying? Or would you regard a speaker's delivery as good if it is so distracting you can't concentrate on the ideas he or she is trying to get across? And, what's the chance that you could be impressed by speakers who show very little interest in their topic or in their audience? Finally, would you pay attention to a speaker who doesn't seem to know very much about his/her topic?

In this section, I'll discuss the five basic dimensions of good delivery. I'm going to refer to these dimensions as "skill areas" in order to emphasize the fact that your skill in each area will be evaluated during the course. Because of the importance of each skill, a minimal degree of competence is necessary in all five areas.

Skill Area 1:   Unobtrusiveness

Some experts regard effective delivery as transparent. This simply means that the audible and visual elements of a speaker's delivery should support rather than draw attention away from the speaker's message. If you're paying attention to the rather bizarre or awkward movements of a speaker, you'll have trouble focusing on the speaker's ideas. While the list of possible distractions is unlimited, there are a few that are common enough to highlight. Consider the following:

Facial Expressions

Some speakers simply aren't aware of what they're doing with their faces while they speak. Others are too nervous to exercise much conscious control. If a speaker's face looks fearful or unnatural, it'll be hard to miss. I remember being distracted by a female student who couldn't stop smiling while giving a very serious speech on how pornography exploits women. I recall another student who couldn't stop raising and lowering his eyebrows.

Bodily Movement

A speaker should move for a reason. Moving to emphasize or illustrate something can be very effective. But a lot of speakers pace back and forth while they talk, rock or sway from side to side, touch their faces, play with their hair, bend their fingers, squeeze their hands together, tap on the lectern, etc. Most of these movements are adaptors which signal the speaker's anxiety. They focus the attention of the speaker and the audience away from the speaker's message to the speaker's nervous symptoms.

Attire

Certainly this is a matter of personal choice and the degree to which clothing and accessories are distracting will depend on the nature of your audience and the strangeness of your appearance. Some experts recommend dressing like those in your audience, just to be on the safe side.

Voice

Vocal quality can be distracting in certain cases. Voices that sound extremely nasal (when vowel sounds are resonated in the nasal cavity), for instance, are considered unpleasant. High pitched voices also are regarded as distracting. In many cases, speech therapy is available to help persons improve the quality of their voices.

Volume

Talking too loud for the size of the room you're in is very distracting. If your listeners are getting a headache, they'll have trouble concentrating on your ideas.

Pronunciation

A foreign accent or an oddly pronounced word is likely to be somewhat distracting to an audience. Yet, my experience is that most students are very supportive of foreign speakers and try extra hard to understand their speeches. Nevertheless, errors in pronunciation can be a notable distraction.

Undoubtedly, this is only a partial list of the potential distractions that can occur when an inexperienced speaker addresses

an audience. In most cases, distractions can be reduced
substantially if we're made aware of them. You may get feedback
from your speech instructor about distracting mannerisms you have.
The best recommendation I can think of is to watch yourself on
videotape.

Skill Area 2: Intelligibility

Good speakers are easy to understand. No matter how hard you
work to avoid distracting your audience, if they can't comprehend
your speech because the words aren't clear you won't be effective.
The most common causes of unintelligible speech are:

Poor Enunciation

The result of either an inability to say certain words because
of the articulatory skill required or an acquired habit of avoiding
the work needed to clearly express certain words, poor enunciation
can make a speaker hard to understand. There are several different
kinds of enunciation problems. The two most common are mumbling and
slurring.

Mumbling results when we fail to properly use our jaw, tongue
or lips to enunciate particular words. Sometimes, parts of a word
are omitted. This often is the case with word endings, especially
words ending in "ing" which might be expressed as, "doin", "workin",
or "goin". Omitting the "st" ending of a word is another common
example as in, "jus" for "just" or "mos" for "most". The middle of
words is also deleted in some cases, such as in the following:

>   "natully" instead of "naturally"
>   "liberry" instead of "library"
>   "goverment" instead of "government"
>   "Febuary" instead of "February"

In addition to omitting part of a word, mumbling can occur when
a speaker substitutes an incorrect sound for the correct sound.
This occurs because the incorrect sound is easier for the speaker to
articulate, not because the speaker doesn't know how to pronounce
the word. Here are some examples:

>   "dis" or "dat" instead of "this" or "that"
>   "git" instead of "get"
>   "fer" instead of "for"
>   "hunderd" instead of "hundred"

Slurring is the second type of enunciation weakness. This occurs when a speaker combines two or more words so that the ending of one word overlaps with the beginning of another. For instance, a speaker might utter the following:

"kinda" instead of "kind of"
"gonnago" instead of "going to go"
"ahdunno" instead of "I don't know"
"whafor" instead of "what for"
"whaddayamean" instead of "what do you mean"

Insufficient Volume

Particularly in a large room, some effort is needed to project your voice so that it is loud enough to be heard by everyone in your audience. Many beginning speakers, unaccustomed to speaking in front of a large group, won't know they are inaudible unless someone says something to them. Most speakers who are hard to hear simply aren't engaging their abdominal muscles enough to carry their voices the necessary distance.

Speaking Too Fast

Speech rate alone is unlikely to interfere with an audience's ability to understand a speaker. The main reason for this is due to the fact that listeners are capable of comprehending speech at a rate substantially faster than ordinary speakers talk. How fast? Some research on "compressed speech" has found that we can understand speech at much more than twice the normal rate--as high as 375 words per minute--while the optimum rate may be as high as 275 wpm (Foulke and Sticht, 1966). But speaking too fast can become a major source of unintelligible speech when the speaker articulates poorly, doesn't talk loud enough, or discusses a topic the audience isn't familiar with.

In most cases, unintelligible speech results from lack of awareness rather than lack of ability. Careless enunciation and inadequate volume can be easily corrected with feedback and practice. While most people are relatively unconcerned about or unaware of such weaknesses, we should realize that things change in a public speaking situation where suddenly all eyes and ears are fixed on everything we do and say. Public speaking is a more formal context than a conversation. And the expectations of listeners tend to be higher as well as their need for speech that is easy to understand. By exerting a little extra effort, most of us can speak

more clearly in such situations if our tendency to mumble or slur is
merely pointed out to us.

Skill Area 3: Fluency

Fluent speech is free of extraneous pauses and common
hesitations such as, "uh" or "uhmm". When we are in situations that
require us to think on our feet without any preparation, such
hesitations are to be expected; they give us time to think. Even
the most intelligent and articulate speakers need to pause
occasionally when they are talking "off the top of their heads."
But, in public speaking situations that allow us time to prepare,
good delivery necessitates fluent speech. Simply stated, the more
prepared we are to give a presentation or the more knowledgeable we
are on a topic, the more fluent our speech will be. Thus, fluency
is a sign of preparation and knowledge. Not surprisingly, speakers
who are fluent are rated as more competent by listeners than
speakers who are not fluent.

Unlike other skill deficiencies that tend to be caused by lack
of awareness on the part of the speaker that the deficiency exists
(i.e., poor enunciation, awkward body movements, inappropriate
facial expressions, soft voice), hesitating or nonfluent speech is
the result of inadequate preparation or practice. My personal
experience in the classroom as an occasional lecturer has taught me
that the more I talk about a particular subject or the more work I
do gathering and organizing my material, the more fluent I'll be
when I speak to a class. So, what's the best way to become a more
fluent speaker? Preparation and practice. I'll talk about how you
should practice a little later.

Skill Area 4: Dynamism

What are the characteristics of a dynamic speaker? The terms
that might be used to describe such a speaker include: energetic,
forceful, enthusiastic, vigorous, animated, expressive, interesting,
captivating, and lively. Certainly these are adjectives we would
use to define "good" delivery. Most of us are capable of speaking
in a dynamic manner and probably all of us have on one occasion or
another. When was the last time you were in a heated argument? Or,
when was the last time you told a good friend about something
fantastic that happened to you? Were you a dynamic speaker in those
situations? Probably.

When we speak in a way that naturally expresses emotion we
become dynamic. The pitch of our voice rises and falls, our face

shows how we feel, our bodies move in a way that reinforces what we say. The problem is that most people are too inhibited or nervous to express emotion in a public speaking context. Nevertheless, dynamism is an essential component of good delivery. It's the only sign we have that lets us know whether speakers care about the subject they are talking about or whether they even understand the importance of what they're saying. Too often, I hear speakers in my classes state shocking statistics about human starvation, alcohol-related traffic fatalities, child abuse, suicide, etc. without any indication that they are concerned about these things.

More often than not, however, beginning speakers are not dynamic simply because they have trouble focusing on the message they want to get across. Rather than being unconcerned about their speech topic, they may find themselves feeling self-conscious and nervous. When you're thinking about performance related things like how you look, how your voice sounds, what the audience is thinking, how much time you have left, etc., it's pretty hard to focus on your ideas. In addition, a lot of beginning speakers who either read too much or memorize too much, end up thinking more about words than ideas. So, what can you do to become a more dynamic speaker? I recommend the following:

1.   Select a speech topic that you are very interested in. If you don't care about your topic, you won't be dynamic. It's too hard to fake.

2.   Use some of the techniques in the chapter on stage fright to cope with your fear. Nervous speakers are more concerned about coping than they are about being dynamic.

3.   You may not be aware that your voice is monotone or that your face is expressionless. Feedback from your instructor might make you aware of the need to speak in a more energetic manner.

Skill Area 5: Directness

Try to imagine yourself walking up to a friend and asking, "How's it going today"? Immediately, your friend pulls out a sheet of paper and starts reading a prepared statement about his/her present physical and emotional state, current interests, plans for the rest of the day, etc. Now I realize that a conversation is not the same thing as a speech. However, most people prefer to be talked TO rather than talked AT under any circumstances. Would you enjoy listening to television news commentators who read their script without ever looking into the camera? Whereas, dynamism shows that a speaker cares about his or her topic, directness shows that a speaker cares about the audience!

Being direct as a speaker means adopting a "conversational" style of speaking in some respects, but not in all respects. As I mentioned earlier when discussing fluency, a speech ought to be different than a conversation in that the speaker should hesitate less. But, there is little need for a classroom speaker to perform in a detached or theatrical manner. Rather, the type of speaking we are interested in, which is called "extemporaneous speaking," requires that the speaker build rapport with his/her audience.

How can you develop a direct style of speaking? There are three things that you can do:

1. Establish eye contact with your audience. Look at individuals in different locations. Hold someone's gaze for a few seconds as you would in a conversation and then do the same thing with someone else in the room. Try to make each person you look at feel as though you are talking directly to them.

2. Use a conversational tone of voice. Except for an attempt to avoid "uh's" and uhmm's", try to sound natural as you would in a conversation. One way to accomplish this style is to avoid memorizing too many words. Another way is to avoid excessive reading. And efforts to over-articulate words should be avoided as well, since they sound artificial.

3. Walk out from behind the lectern occasionally. Standing behind the lectern for the entire presentation could make you appear distant and overly formal. Moving away from the lectern to demonstrate something or to simply accent a transition in your speech is a very effective way to psychologically, as well as physically, get closer to your audience.

To briefly review, a speaker will have a good delivery when he or she is unobtrusive, intelligible, fluent, dynamic, and direct. While these skills are characteristic of effective speaking in any situation, they are fundamental when developing competence in extemporaneous speaking. What is extemporaneous speaking? That's what I'll discuss in the next section.

DEVELOPING A GOOD DELIVERY

The public speaking course you are taking is a course in extemporaneous speaking. This kind of speaking is typical of most situations in which people stand up and talk and can be characterized as follows:

1. The speaker has time to prepare and practice.
2. The speaker develops and uses notes in the form of an outline.
3. The speaker talks to the audience in a direct manner.

Of course, there are other ways of speaking in public. One method is called impromptu speaking. The primary difference between impromptu and extemporaneous speaking is the amount of preparation that is allowed. When you are asked on the spur of the moment to stand up and "say a few words" you will end up giving an impromptu speech if you accept the invitation. Another method is referred to as manuscript speaking and consists of reading the speech from a completely written manuscript rather than using an outline as in extemporaneous speaking. The final method is memorized speaking. Speaking without the use of notes whatsoever, this kind of speaking is limited mainly to competitive speech contests or other kinds of performance contexts. In some situations however, as when we must prepare a very short speech in advance (i.e., 2-3 minutes), memorized speeches can be effective if delivered in a "spontaneous" sounding manner.

All of the methods mentioned above have advantages and disadvantages. But since we believe more strongly in the need for training in extemporaneous speaking than in the other methods, this course is designed to help you become a more skilled extemporaneous speaker. If, in the near or distant future, you need to give an oral presentation, it is not likely to be one in which you'll need to memorize, recite, or speak without any advance notice.

With adequate preparation and practice, it shouldn't be too difficult to deliver extemporaneously a four to six minute speech, as you will need to do in this course. Here are some tips in response to often asked questions.

Should I Memorize Any Part of the Speech?

Unlike a memorized speech, an extemporaneous presentation allows, and in fact, encourages limited use of notes. The aim is to achieve some balance between memorizing everything and reading everything. But the need to avoid distracting pauses and insufficient eye contact means that you'll have to know what you want to say and how you're going to say it. You should try to commit the following things to memory:

1. Your introduction and conclusion. In a four to six minute speech it shouldn't be too hard to memorize these parts of your speech. An important function of your introduction and conclusion is to catch the attention of your audience. That's difficult to do if you need to keep looking at your notes. Some students begin their speeches by telling stories, relating personal experiences, describing imaginary situations, etc. Reading these things can greatly reduce their emotional impact.

2. The main sequence of your ideas. The reason for this is so that occasionally you can move on to your "next point" without looking at your notes.

3. Explanations of some main points. After signposting a heading in your outline, you should be able to discuss it briefly before looking at your notes again. But, you should memorize the basic idea underlying what you want to say rather than the exact wording of the idea.

What Kind of Notes Should I Use?

Although notes are encouraged in an extemporaneous speech, they must be very limited. Your instructor may not allow you to use more than a single index card to deliver your speech. Bringing up a lot of notes encourages you to avoid looking at your audience. Some guidelines concerning notes are:

Don't Clutter Your Note Card With Too Many Words.

Use a key word outline so that the words "trigger" in your mind what you want to say next. Be sure the words are easy to see.

Don't Write On More Than One Side of a Card.

If you do you could find yourself turning it over only to find something you've already talked about on the other side.

Hold the Card In Your Hand While You Speak.

A small index card is unobtrusive enough not to interfere with your eye contact when you bring it up to your face to look at. Don't set it down on a table. At best, you'll need to look down too often; at worst, you'll forget where you put the card.

Try To Anticipate When You'll Need To Look At Your Notes Again.

By doing this you can look at your notes while you're still speaking thus avoiding the need for a lengthy pause.

What Should I Do With My Body While I'm Speaking?

Students who ask this question often want to know whether or not to stand behind a table or lectern, what they should do with their hands, if its OK to lean back on a table, how often or when they should move to another spot in the room, etc. Here are some recommendations:

Movement Should Be Purposeful.

That means you should try to minimize movement that does nothing more than distract your listeners. Gesture to emphasize or illustrate something. Move to another point in the room to demonstrate something, to discuss a visual aid, or to focus attention on movement from one idea to another.

Don't Stand Behind A Lectern Unless Absolutely Necessary.

While my feelings are not as strong, there are some good reasons to follow such advice. Beginning speakers standing behind a lectern or table find it hard to resist the temptation to lean on it, to tap it with their fingers, or to needlessly clutch it--all very distracting. Also, it's more difficult to build rapport with an audience when you're standing behind a table or lectern and more difficult to be dynamic (i.e., it's harder to gesture behind a huge lectern than away from it).

How Should I Practice My Speech?

Even if for no other reason, you must practice your speech in order to make sure you'll stick to the time limit that's been

imposed. If you haven't had a lot of experience giving
presentations, one of the most immediate and striking things you'll
discover is how unpredictable the passage of time can be. A lot of
students say they can't believe how fast it goes by; others feel
that six minutes is longer than a lifetime. In any event, you don't
want to find yourself in the awkward position of being in the middle
of your speech when your time runs out. Nor do you want to be
"wrapping it up" with more than three out of a possible six minutes
still remaining.

1.   Go through your speaking outline in your head several
      times to see how it "sounds" to you. Imagine yourself
      giving the speech.

2.   Stand up and actually give the speech. You might want to
      look in a mirror or tape it, so you can get some
      audio-visual feedback. The feedback will allow you to
      find out if your style is unobtrusive, intelligible,
      fluent, dynamic, and direct.

3.   If you think you are weak in one or more skill areas (i.e.
      you're not very dynamic), then work on practicing to
      improve that particular skill.

4.   Deliver the speech to a friend and ask for some feedback.

                              SUMMARY

     In this chapter we've explored the delivery or nonverbal
communication of a public speaker. Delivery consists of various
audible behaviors that result from the multiple processes of
respiration, phonation resonation and articulation. These behaviors
include: pitch, quality, volume, articulation, pronunciation, and
rate. But delivery also includes an array of visual behaviors. The
physical movement of a speaker consists of: emblems, adaptors,
illustrators, affect displays, and regulators. And physical
appearance includes the way a speaker looks and dresses.

     We often think of a speaker's delivery as something independent
of his or her speech content. But, as we've seen, delivery and
content are interrelated. A speaker's delivery can substitute for,
repeat, emphasize, contradict, or complement the verbal message
being conveyed.

     The section in this chapter on the dimensions of good delivery
focused on five distinct skill areas--each being crucial to the
delivery of a speaker. Good delivery means not distracting your

audience (unobtrusive), being easy to understand (intelligible), being sufficiently prepared to speak without a lot of useless pauses (fluent), showing that you are involved in your topic (dynamic), and showing that you care about your audience (direct).

While this is a course in extemporaneous speaking, you should be aware that other kinds of public speaking situations can call for an impromptu, memorized, or manuscript speech. But extemporaneous speaking is, by far, the most common type of public speaking. To aid you in your attempt to develop skill in extemporaneous speaking, a number of useful guidelines were presented that addressed common questions asked by students in introductory speech classes regarding the memory, use of notes, movement, and practice.

Chapter Seven

Persuasive Argumentation

By

Robert Trapp

Humans use speech for a variety of reasons and one of the most
important is to persuade each other to adopt certain beliefs or to
take certain actions. Public speaking is only one of many forums
for persuasion in our society. In interpersonal communication
situations, persuasion occurs when relational partners work to
improve their relationships, when college roommates struggle to
adapt to one another, or when co-workers attempt to divide their
tasks fairly.

Still, public speaking is an important medium of persuasion.
In face-to-face public speaking situations, citizens address city
council members to encourage them to support issues like a new
school building, ministers try to impress values on audiences,
lawyers try to win convictions or acquittals, and business people
try to persuade each other to make decisions relevant to their
businesses. In mass-mediated public speaking situations, automobile
dealers try to sell their wares, celebrities try to raise funds for
their favorite causes, and politicians try to win elections.

Persuasion has a reputation that is not above reproach. In
fact, some people consider the process of persuasion inherently
unethical. Their reasoning goes like this: One of the unique
qualities of a human is the ability and right to make free choices.
Persuasion is the attempt by one person to interfere with the free
choice of another. Therefore, we have no right to try to persuade
others to do things that they would not do of their own free will.

While this argument is not without merit, anyone who thinks for
one minute that we could eliminate persuasion from modern society is

extremely naive. Persuasion is endemic to our society. Our choices are to ignore the phenomena or to try to understand and practice it in ethical ways. Those who decide to ignore persuasion because it is inherently unethical, leave themselves unprotected against those persons whose ethic of persuasion is their belief that the ends justify the means. Only by deciding to try to understand the process of persuasion, can we protect ourselves against the unscrupulous, while at the same time, devising methods of persuasion that treat our fellow citizen as a person not as an object.

The fact that we do not expand on the issue of the ethics of persuasion, should not be construed to indicate that we think the topic is unimportant. To the contrary, this is one of the most difficult issues with which scholars of persuasion deal. Still, an extended treatment of this issue is beyond the scope of this text. For those interested in pursuing this worthwhile topic, we suggest Richard Johannessen's excellent work entitled Ethics in Human Communication.

In this chapter, we will discuss two sources and one roadblock to persuasion. While both the speaker and argumentation are important sources of persuasion, all of our efforts to persuade may be unsuccessful if we fail to attend to defensiveness as a major roadblock to persuasion.

THE SPEAKER AS A SOURCE OF PERSUASION

The idea that speakers, apart from any arguments they advance, are important to persuasion is not a new one. In classical times, this concept was called ethos. In his Rhetoric, Aristotle took note of the importance of ethos in speaking: "Of the modes of persuasion furnished by the spoken word there are three kinds. The first kind depends on the personal character of the speaker." Current research has confirmed this point of view.

Effects of Source Credibility

In their summary of research on source credibility, Kenneth Andersen and Theodore Clevenger Jr. noted that "the finding is almost universal that the ethos of the source is related in some way to the impact of the message. This generalization applies not only to political, social, religious, and economic issues, but also to matters of aesthetic judgment and personal taste" (pp 77).

One interesting aspect about the relationship between source credibility and persuasion involves the concept of time. In their classic study of source credibility, Carl I. Hovland and Walter Weiss (1951-52) found that a source with high credibility produces significantly more <u>immediate</u> attitude change than a source with low credibility. When attitude change was measured one month later, they found that the amount of attitude change created by the source of low credibility had increased while the attitude change created by the source of high credibility had decreased. This reversal was so significant that after one month, the amount of attitude change created by the two sources was approximately the same.

Hovland and Weiss call this reversal of attitude change the "sleeper effect." They attributed the cause of the sleeper effect to an audience's tendency to forget the source of the message. While they presented persuasive evidence to support their argument, later we will consider an alternate explanation of the problem that provides means for a speaker to try to combat the sleeper effect.

Dimensions of Source Credibility

What do we mean when we say Randall is a credible speaker? Does this mean he possesses some single, magical characteristic that causes others to believe what he says? Probably not. Source credibility is more complicated than that. It is composed, not of one, but of several dimensions. Even Aristotle realized that source credibility (or <u>ethos</u>) was not a unidimensional concept. He wrote that "there are <u>three</u> things that inspire confidence in the orator's own character--the three, namely, that induce us to believe a thing apart from any proof of it: good sense, good moral character, and good will."

Since that time, social scientists have attempted to clarify the dimensions of source credibility. No clear answer exists at this time, since different studies have produced different results (See Thompson, 60-61 for a summary of these studies). In general, three dimensions seem to be the most stable across studies. These dimensions are competence, trustworthiness, and dynamism.

The competence dimension of source credibility involves the audience's perception of whether or not the speaker is knowledgeable about the subject matter. So, an audience might judge Sara as a competent speaker if she is perceived as an expert on her topic. The trustworthiness dimension, as the name implies, involves whether or not the audience perceives the speaker as a truthful and sincere person. The stereotype of the used-car salesperson is of someone with low credibility due to a lack of trustworthiness. The dynamism dimension, while more illusive, refers to whether or not the audience perceives the speaker to be dynamic, active, and energetic.

So, a variety of dimensions contribute to an audience's perception of a speaker's credibility. In the language of classical persuasion, a person of good sense, good will, and good moral character is high in credibility. In the language of modern communication theory, a credible speaker is competent, trustworthy, and dynamic.

Manipulating Your Credibility

To a certain extent, our credibility is a function of the person we are and the experiences we have had. But, what if your name isn't Paul Samuelson, but you still want to give a talk about economics? What if you don't have the international negotiation experience of Henry Kissinger, but you think you have something to say about the subject? Is there anything you can do? Fortunately, the answer is yes.

In the paragraphs that follow, we will outline some suggestions for improving your chances of being perceived as a credible speaker. While most of these suggestions are speculative, our experience tells us they are workable. Of course, as with most communication variables, the context in which these techniques are used needs to be considered with care.

Presenting Yourself as a Competent Person

While some people have better credentials than others, almost everyone can benefit from presenting themselves to an audience in the best light possible. Additionally, even people with impeccable credentials will be called on, from time to time, to speak in situations where their credentials are unknown. In both of these situations speakers need to know how to present themselves in ways that will lead audiences to view them as competent as possible. A few of these ways are:

Have Someone Introduce You

Having someone well known to the audience introduce you and tell the audience what a wonderfully brilliant individual you really are, has obvious advantages over performing this immodest task yourself. Seasoned public speakers will usually approach the person in charge of the speaking engagement and say something like, "Who will be introducing me?" The conversation then goes something like this:

"Well?? I really dunno? Ah? I guess I will."
"Great. Do you need a few facts about me?"
"Sure--That would help me lots."

At this point, the speaker presents the newly found introducer with a very immodest introduction written, of course, by the speaker. Then, while the introducer is explaining how the speaker is the most esteemed person in the entire field, the speaker sits to the side and blushes modestly. Then, the speaker rises and says "Wow!! With an introduction like that, I'm almost afraid to begin." Of course this account is exaggerated, but it explains the benefits of having another person say things about you that you have greater difficulty saying about yourself.

Present Your Qualifications or Experience Yourself

Of course, at times, we will be called on to speak when we have to do the dirty job of introducing ourself. This is a more difficult situation since it requires that you find a way to present your qualifications and experience without sounding overly immodest. Some of your qualifications can easily be presented in the introduction to your speech, while others may be woven into the fabric of the speech.

Quote Respected Authorities

In situations where you may not have extensive credentials yourself, you can enhance your credibility in the eyes of your audience by citing authorities who are respected in the field. When you quote highly qualified authorities, the credibility that those speakers have is at least partially transferred to you.

Be Consistent

When a speaker appears to be inconsistent in the use of facts or arguments, an audience is not likely to perceive the speaker as competent. So, extra care to avoid appearing inconsistent is worth the effort.

Presenting Yourself as a Trustworthy Person

Audiences expect speakers to be trustworthy as well as competent. In fact, trustworthiness may be more important than competence with respect to certain topics. So, what can a speaker do to put forward an image as a trustworthy person?

Treat the Topic From the Audience's Perspective

The issues about which we attempt to persuade one another are problematic ones--issues about which reasonable people can disagree. If these issues were unproblematic, persuasion would be unnecessary. Even though you may believe strongly and sincerely in your point of view, you should realize that it is not the only legitimate point of view. Making a sincere effort to see the issue from the audience's point of view and communicating that effort to your audience is an important step toward presenting yourself as a trustworthy speaker.

Our primary difficulty seems to stem from the fact that many of us become so ego-involved in our topics that we are unable to see any perspective other than our own. Rather than going to the trouble of trying to understand other perspectives, we tend to characterize people who hold them as ignorant or stupid. When we are able to step outside of our own egocentric point of view and make a reasonable effort to see the other side of the issue, we increase the chances that our audience will perceive us as credible speakers.

Thus, speakers need to make every effort to view the subject from their audiences point of view and try to determine what arguments will be persuasive from the point of view of the audience. And, they need to try to adapt their speech to that perspective.

Present Both Sides

A trustworthy speaker not only shows understanding of, but respect for, the point of view of the audience. One of the best ways to communicate this respect is to present both sides of the topic. And, once we are able to recognize and respect the opposite point of view, this becomes a much less difficult task.

For example, a speaker who is arguing against capital punishment should try to understand and respect the outrage that the audience holds for murderers and rapists. And, the speaker should include arguments that express this outrage in the speech. Surely, being against capital punishment does not entail being sympathetic to murderers and rapists. And, the speaker needs to make sure that the audience understands this point.

Presenting Yourself as a Dynamic Person

Having done everything you can do to present yourself as competent and trustworthy, the matter of dynamism still remains. Perhaps one of the things we remember most about great speakers is, how dynamic they are. So, what can you do to present yourself as a dynamic person? While much of the material in the chapter on delivery is relevant to this point, we will suggest a couple of strategies here.

Be Physically Energetic

Speakers who immediately grab the lectern and turns loose only when the speech is finished are no more likely to be perceived as dynamic than the speaker who moves around like a caged lion. A dynamic speaker is an energetic speaker who is not frozen to notes or to a lectern but whose movements are meaningful.

Practice Your Delivery

At the very least, give your speech in front of a full length mirror so you can get a better idea of how an audience might perceive you. If you have the opportunity, have someone videotape your speech so you can watch it. Where delivery is concerned, you will be your own best critic.

ARGUMENTATION AS A SOURCE OF PERSUASION

Although you, as a speaker, are an excellent source of persuasion, you will not be able to persuade an audience unless you are prepared with sound and convincing arguments. While the field of argumentation includes much more than how to present persuasive arguments, we will limit ourselves to a discussion of this feature of argumentation.

Furthermore, we will limit ourselves to what has been called "informal" as opposed to "formal" argumentation. Formal argumentation (also called formal or symbolic logic) is a special area of philosophy concerned with the study of deduction. Many argumentation scholars became disillusioned with formal logic since it did not seem relevant to the everyday world of controversy. That disillusionment has lead to the development of a field called informal logic or ordinary argumentation. Since we are interested in developing argumentation skills that are relevant to our everyday lives in areas like business, education, and civic affairs, we will emphasize the informal, as opposed to the formal, theories of argumentation.

1958 was a watershed year in the study of argumentation. In that year, two major works were produced; one in England and one in Belgium, that have since lead to an increased emphasis on the study of how arguments are presented in everyday life. That year, the British philosopher Stephen Toulmin published a work entitled, Uses of Argument, while Belgian philosophers Chaim Perelman and Lucie Olbrechts-Tyteca published the results of their ten-year study in a two-volume work entitled, La Nouvelle Rhetorique: Traite de l'Argumentation. Their theory, which became known as "the new rhetoric" was translated to English in 1969. Although these two works were produced independently, they were both to become very influential in the development of theories of argumentation relevant to persuasion in everyday life.

Toulmin's Uses of Argument is most well known for his layout of an argument. In the next section, we will use the basics of his layout to sketch a model that we think is useful for constructing an argument. We will then use ideas borrowed from Perelman and Olbrechts-Tyteca (namely audience and argument techniques) to embellish and complete the model.

A Model for Developing an Argument

As we have said, our model for developing an argument is not original. We have borrowed all of its component parts from others and simply combined their ideas into a system that we find useful. The elements we will use to explain this model are (1) the layout of an argument, (2) evidence, and (3) argumentation techniques.

The Layout of an Argument

We have decided to utilize the Toulmin layout of argument as the basis for our model, not because we think it is an adequate descriptive model, but because we think it is a useful tool for discussing various components of an argument. The layout of an argument is based on a metaphor of motion. An argument involves movement from evidence to a claim. Thus, making an argument is like taking a trip, since we start somewhere and are trying to go somewhere else. Toulmin's layout involves six interrelated concepts but, for the sake of simplicity, we will deal only with the three that he considered indispensible.

The first component is called the claim. The claim is the conclusion we are trying to justify. In the movement metaphor, it is the destination of the trip. The claim is the answer to the question "Where are we going?" Toulmin called the second component "grounds" or "data", but for simplicity, we will call it evidence. Evidence consists of facts or other data on which the argument is based. In our metaphor it answers the question, "What do we have to go on?" Toulmin called the third component of an argument the warrant and we will call it the argumentation technique. In our metaphor, it answers the question "What road do you take to get from this starting point to that destination? The argumentation technique answers the question "How do you justify the move from this evidence to that claim? These three components are the primary elements of an argument.

The basic layout of an argument can be displayed as follows:

FIGURE ONE

THE LAYOUT OF AN ARGUMENT

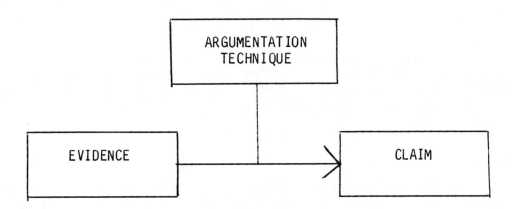

To illustrate, a speaker, arguing that the U.S. should adopt a mandatory seatbelt law, might begin with the evidence that Canada's adoption of a mandatory seatbelt law caused the rate of seatbelt usage to grow from 20% to 85%. The speaker would then argue that since citizens of the USA and Canada are alike in their propensity to obey the law, a similar experience could be expected in the USA. Thus, the speaker has produced a claim that shows a mandatory seatbelt law would substantially increase seatbelt usage in the US.

Such an argument is illustrated in figure two:

FIGURE TWO

THE LAYOUT OF AN ARGUMENT USING AN EXAMPLE

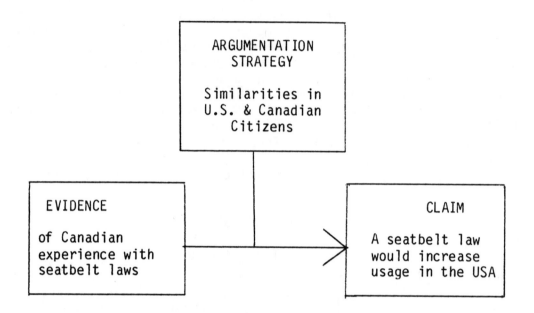

So, this is the basic layout of an argument. We have only presented a skeletal outline of the layout, but it should be sufficient for our purposes here. In the sections that follow, we will put the flesh on the skeleton.

Evidence

The foundation of an argument is evidence. Without solid evidence for support, an argument cannot be sound no matter how reasonable it appears. In this section, we will consider several types of evidence and some general tests that can be used to evaluate each type.

Types of Evidence.

A variety of systems have been used for the classification of evidence. No single theoretical system has ever been accepted as the best system. For our purposes, we will divide evidence into two general categories: real and personal.

Real evidence is defined by Douglas Ehninger and Wayne Brockriede as "things that can be seen, heard, tasted, or touched--things immediately perceptible to one or more of the senses" (55). Real evidence is frequently used in criminal trials. The video tapes of the defendants robbing the bank, the fingerprints on the murder weapon, or the article of clothing found in the home of the victim are all examples of real evidence.

Real evidence can also be used in other public speaking situations as well. When President Reagan displayed captured weapons to justify a military invasion, he was using real evidence. A student's speech on nuclear power that included a dramatic demonstration of the disposal of radioactive materials used real evidence. Another student, who argued in favor of a particular theory of evolution, brought fossils to class as evidence of the way a particular species evolved.

Personal evidence is the second general category of evidence. Whereas, real evidence consists of things that are immediately perceptible to the senses of the audience, personal evidence consists of data not physically present but reported by another person. Because human reports of evidence are so much more available than real evidence, this type of evidence is more frequently used in public speaking situations.

Personal evidence usually takes one of three forms. One kind of personal evidence consists of reported facts. Reported facts are similar to real evidence except the audience does not have physical access to the data. Whereas, in the case of real evidence the audience actually saw the weapons that were captured by U.S. forces; in the case of personal evidence, the speaker quoted a newspaper reporter's description of the weapons cache. Instead of displaying fossils, the person using personal evidence cited reports of a famous archeological dig. Although perhaps not as persuasive as real evidence, when properly used, reported facts can also be convincing.

A second kind of personal evidence is statistical data. Two types of statistical data are often useful in speaking. As the name implies, descriptive statistics are numerical calculations that represent certain characteristics of a group. Descriptive statistics are useful when presentation of factual evidence relevant to every case would be impossible. While they could not possibly present factual evidence about every person, the National Organization for the Reform of Marijuana Laws presents statistical data that each of 2.5 million Americans grow an average of 3.5 pounds of marijuana for their personal use. To the extent that the data were gathered according to adequate procedures, this descriptive statistic is useful in constructing an argument.

A second kind of statistic is called an inferential statistic. This statistic allows us to draw inferences or make predictions on the basis of statistical data. Suppose that one needs to know the average SAT score of students graduating in the upper 10% of their high school class. Gathering that data would be a monumental and expensive task, but by gathering a random sample of students in the upper 10% and calculating inferential statistics one can infer the average score of the entire population. Of course, both descriptive and inferential statistics are very useful in public speaking.

A third form of personal evidence is called testimony. By testimony, we are referring to opinions and explanations offered by experts in the field. None of us can expect to be able to understand everything about every issue of importance to us. As a result, we must depend on experts in the field to guide our opinion. If you are concerned about the effects of nuclear power production on our environment but are not a nuclear physicist, you may be in a position where you are forced to rely on the judgment of experts. For this reason, expert testimony is very useful in public speaking situations.

Speakers use personal testimony for a variety of reasons. Sometimes, the details of evidence needed to establish an argument are so complicated that one cannot possibly explain the point in the time available. In this case, personal testimony may be useful. In other situations, a speaker may use the testimony of an expert to show that experts in the field agree with the speaker on some important aspect of the topic. Whatever the reason, expert testimony should be selected with care.

Tests of Evidence.

As we discuss tests of evidence relevant to the various types of evidence, we want to stress the fact that no completely objective tests of evidence exist. In fact, the strength of evidence is ultimately a judgment to be made by an audience. When we suggest a certain test that can be applied to a certain type of evidence, we need to stress the fact that all tests are not applied by all audiences. Still, a careful speaker will select evidence that can stand the scrutiny of the most skeptical audience.

Tests of Real Evidence. Obviously, real evidence, when available, can be especially persuasive. Still, audiences can apply some tests to real evidence. Two tests are particularly applicable to real evidence (Ehninger and Brockriede, p. 58). The first test, concerning the authenticity of the evidence, is relevant to our earlier examples. Is the person shown in the video-tape actually the defendant? Were the displayed weapons actually donated by the USSR? Are the fossils authentic? So, while real evidence is especially persuasive, its authenticity can still be called into question.

The second test concerns whether the evidence is typical of the class it is said to represent. Perhaps the fossils are authentic, but are they typical of the geological period under discussion.

Tests of Personal Evidence.

Personal evidence can be subjected to a variety of tests. Here are some tests that apply to various types of personal evidence.

Tests of reported facts. A skeptical audience may raise several questions about reported factual evidence. These questions have to do with the nature of the observer, the nature of the observation, and the reporting of the observation. First, concerns about the nature of the observer include questions, such as, "Was the observer physically and mentally able to observe the event?" and "Did the observer have the experience and training to interpret the event properly?" If a speaker used the testimony of someone who claimed to have been visited by green Martians to prove the existence of extra-terrestrial life, even a not-too-skeptical audience might question the physical and/or mental state of the observer of the event. The question of the professional experience and training is relevant to the factual evidence reported by an archeologist.

Second, concerns about the nature of the observation include questions, such as, "Under what conditions was the observation made?" Were the green Martians observed in the light of day or in the foggy swamps of Louisiana. Could the observer have mistaken ordinary human beings in the swamp for Martians? Another issue involves the question, "Were the conditions at the time of the observation similar to the conditions of today?" Had the President of the United States displayed a weapons cache that was captured many years prior to the invasion when a different government was in power? A skeptical audience ought to question the relevance of reported facts to the current situation.

Tests of statistics. Statistical evidence has become an extremely important source of persuasive evidence in our society. All too frequently, audiences fail to ask critical questions about

statistical evidence. Still, a critical audience will keep a
variety of questions in mind. While a comprehensive treatment of
the validity of statistical data is beyond the scope of this
chapter, we will mention several tests that a skeptical audience
will apply to the statistical data.

First, is the statistic appropriate to the question? Remember
that every statistic is a means of presenting data from a particular
perspective and that in illuminating some aspect of a body of data a
statistic may simultaneously hide other aspects of the same data.
So, while our knowledge of the average (mean) SAT score of high
school students in the upper 10% of their graduating class may tell
us something about the central tendency of that group, it tells us
nothing about the range of scores in that group. Thus, we need to
remember to choose statistical units with care.

Second, are adequate sampling techniques employed? Since
inferential statistics are used to make a claim about a population
based on some characteristic of a sample, the sampling technique is
very important. Speakers should be careful when selecting
statistical evidence to make sure that evidence they selected was
gathered using appropriate sampling techniques.

Third, are the statistics current? Statistics are frequently
used to describe a situation as it exists at the current period of
time. One should then ask whether or not the statistics are recent
enough so they can accurately account for current affairs. While
the fact that statistics are not current does not necessarily
indicate they are inappropriate, one should take care to make sure
that the period of time covered by the statistic is similar to the
period of time they are intended to describe.

Fourth, are the concepts compared by the statistics relevant to
the question? The interpretation of statistical evidence is often
more important than technical aspects of the statistic. Are the
concepts about which claims are made, similar to the concept that
was actually measured by the statistic? For instance, a major brand
of toothpaste advertises that their brand of toothpaste is better at
preventing cavities than the same toothpaste without fluoride. The
main claim of the commercial is that their brand is better than
other brands at preventing cavities than other brands. What their
statistics really prove is that fluoride toothpaste is better than
non-fluoride toothpaste; not that one brand of fluoride toothpaste
is better than another.

Tests of testimony. One very important aspect of expert
testimony concerns the source of testimony. Some of the following
questions should be asked when selecting testimony as evidence.

First, is the source qualified to testify about this particular question? Although Albert Einstein is highly qualified to speak about physics, he would not be a particularly persuasive source to cite on the topic of macro-economics. Similarly we would not quote Paul Samuelson if we were giving a speech on the nature of the universe. Second, what are the motives of the source? What are the motives of the person who is being quoted? Testimony given by a person without prior motives is much more persuasive than testimony given too willingly. Although Henry Kissinger is highly qualified in the field of foreign policy, his direct participation in the Vietnam war may cause some audiences to suspect his views on the subject.

Before concluding this section on evidence, we would be remiss if we did not clarify one important aspect about evidence. Evidence is symbolic, not physical. If we were only referring to personal evidence, this point would be so obvious as to be trivial. What we mean is that all evidence, real and personal, becomes evidence when and only when humans agree it is evidence. Not only do humans decide when some fact constitutes evidence, they decide the degree to which evidence is relevant and believable.

In public speaking situations, this means that audience considerations are of paramount importance when a speaker selects evidence. What are the odds that the audience will agree that this fact is evidence for that claim? What are the odds that the audience will find this evidence persuasive? Although we talk about tests of evidence as though they were objective standards for the evaluation of evidence, we need to constantly remind ourselves that acceptance by an audience is the real test of evidence.

Argumentation Techniques

Although evidence forms the foundation of an argument, the technique of argumentation is an equally important consideration. The notions of evidence and argumentation techniques are usually interrelated. Sometimes, the choice of evidence dictates the argumentation technique that one will follow; sometimes the choice of an argumentation technique necessitates the location of certain kinds of evidence.

Although our classification of argumentation techniques is somewhat different, we nevertheless depend heavily on the theory of Chaim Perelman. We will organize the techniques of argumentation into five categories. All but the final category depend on what Perelman calls "liaison" or the process of gaining an audience's acceptance of our claim by linking that claim to some evidence. The final technique is called dissociation and is used to avoid the appearance of incompatibility.

Quasi-Logical Arguments.

The first category of argument techniques is similar in form to formal logic. In fact, much of their persuasiveness can be traced to their similarity to formal logic.

One example of a quasi-logical argument is an argument of reciprocity. Such a strategy is useful when we want to show how two things are similar. So one could argue that capital punishment is a just punishment for the crime of murder since the punishment so nearly fits the crime. "An eye for an eye, a tooth for a tooth" is an example of the argument of reciprocity.

Another example of the usefulness of a quasi-logical argument occurs when you need to show that your audience ought to agree with you in order to avoid an incompatibility. Just as philosophers believe in the law of non-contradiction, people believe that their attitudes and beliefs should be compatible with one another. A speaker uses this argumentation strategy by showing the audience how their belief in abortion is incompatible with their belief in the sanctity of human life.

Argumentation By Association, the second kind of argumentation strategy, can take several forms but the most important for our purposes is the cause and effect argument. A speaker needs this type of argument strategy frequently in persuasive speaking since a determination of cause and effect often is needed before one can suggest solutions to problems.

Arguments about cause and effect are difficult to establish since causes are rarely (philosophers say never) observable. So a cause must be inferred from its association with the supposed effect. One might argue, for instance, that smoking cigarettes causes lung cancer by showing the association between smoking and cancer. Strong associations like this one can be demonstrated in three ways: First, by demonstrating that the cause is associated with the effect (people who smoke have higher than average rates of lung cancer); second, by demonstrating that the absence of the cause is associated with the absence of the effect (people who do not smoke have lower than average rates of lung cancer); and third, by demonstrating a statistical correlation between the cause and the effect (the risk of lung cancer is proportional to the number of cigarettes smoked). Even when one is careful, establishing a cause and effect relationship is difficult. So we need to take special

care with this difficult but important type of argumentation
strategy.

Argumentation By Example.

The third type of strategy actually includes argument by
example and illustration. Examples involve the use of several
specific cases that have some element in common. The arguer then
claims that this element is common, not only to the specific
examples, but to other cases in the same class. So, the speaker
interested in demonstrating how U.S. allies are using torture might
show examples of torture in Guatemala, El Salvador, and Chili. The
speaker then would claim that torture is a general practice among
most of our South and Central American allies.

Another form of argument by example is illustration. Whereas,
a speaker using argument by example typically uses several instances
to make a point, a speaker using illustration as an argument
strategy usually presents one extended example. The purpose of an
illustration is not to prove the argument but to make it especially
vivid in the mind of the audience. So, a speaker might select a
specific case of torture and present it with such vividness that it
overshadows everything else.

An especially persuasive way to use this argumentation strategy
is to combine several short examples with one extended illustration.
This speaker might start with the illustration to make the topic of
torture especially important for the audience. After the
illustration has made torture vivid, the speaker would claim that
this was not an isolated or atypical example, and give several short
examples of different forms of torture in different countries. So,
by using argument by example, in these two forms, a speaker attempts
to establish a general rule on the basis of specific examples.

The persuasiveness of this argument strategy depends on several
factors such as the number of examples used and whether the audience
believes that the examples are typical. Skeptical members of the
audience may be asking themselves whether the reports of torture are
isolated instances or whether they are a part of the general
practice of South and Central American Governments. They may also
be asking if the countries are typical of other governments in the
region. The persuasive speaker would do well to anticipate these
kinds of questions and provide information in the speech to deal
with them.

Argument By Analogy.

The fourth category is based on the process of comparing knowns
and unknowns. An analogy is usually developed by comparing two
parallel cases both of which are alike in several known ways. We
also have observed that the first case possesses a certain
characteristic that we have not observed in the second case.
Arguing by analogy is the process of inferring that the second case
also possesses that characteristic.

Say, for example, that we want to convince an audience that the
government in Nicaragua is ripe for domination by the USSR. We
might begin the analogy by talking about the similarities between
Cuba and Nicaragua--how the USSR convinced the Cubans that the U.S.
was the enemy and that communism was the best solution to the
problem of poverty in their country and how the USSR is now
preaching the same message to the Nicaraguans. We would then show
how the techniques used by the USSR to alienate Cuba from the USA
are now being applied in Nicaragua. Then, we would try to convince
our audience that communism is likely to succeed in Nicaragua (the
unknown) just like it has in Cuba (the known).

An analogy is an extended metaphor. Metaphorically, we might
say that Nicaragua is the Cuba of the 1980's. To produce a
full-fledged analogy we expand the metaphor as we have demonstrated
in the preceding paragraph. Argument by analogy is especially
persuasive since metaphor is such a common aspect of ordinary
language. Still, a skeptical audience will be listening to
determine whether the similarities between the two cases are
sufficient to make the presence of the unknown characteristic a
sufficiently high probability. Providing a clear answer to this
question is the key to convincing a skeptical audience.

Argument By Dissociation.

The final category is designed to help a speaker avoid the
appearance of incompatibility. You may recall that, earlier, we
used the quasi-logical argument to create the appearance of an
incompatibility between an audience's belief in abortion and their
belief in the sanctity of life. Say an audience perceives that the
speaker is faced with this type of incompatibility. The speaker can
use argument by dissociation as a technique to avoid the
incompatibility.

In order to deal with this incompatibility, the speaker divides
one of the two concepts (the sanctity of life and abortion) into two
other concepts. One of the new concepts represents reality and the
other represents the appearance of reality. So in this case the

speaker might say that the sanctity of life is really two concepts not one: life and _human_ life. The sanctity of life is not really an important value; it only appears to be so. The reason we know that life in general is not valuable is that, in the nature of things, we must destroy other life to survive. Humans eat vegetables which are alive. Humans eat other living animals. No one gets particularly upset when someone else eats coleslaw or a Big Mac, but these acts destroy the life of the cabbage and the cow. What we really value is not life in general but human life. Having created the two concepts, the speaker is left with the task of showing how the act of abortion is a termination of life in general but not human life. Of course, a variety of strategies are available to make this argument. If this strategy succeeds, the audience may be convinced that the positions held by the speaker are no longer incompatible.

The argument by dissociation is useful in a variety of cases where the issue concerns not so much the values associated with your proposal but other values that your audience believes and construes as incompatible with your proposal. For instance, the failure of the ERA to gain acceptance is not attributable to the fact that people are against equality so much as it was that they feared the ERA was incompatible with other important values. So the ERA failed because its proponents were unable to dissociate the ERA from issues surrounding bathrooms and bedrooms.

These five strategies are conceptual devices that you can use to develop arguments to support positions on any variety of issues. Of course, the fact that a certain argumentation strategy was followed to the letter does not mean the argument will ultimately prove acceptable to a skeptical audience. In the next section we will discuss some standards that audiences use to separate good arguments from bad ones.

Differentiating Good Argument From Bad Argument

As we have stressed several times, audiences decide when an argument is good or bad. In this section, we will clarify the notion of audience and discuss some standards they may apply.

The Idea of an Audience

We agree with Perelman that an argument implies the existence of an audience. No one would write a book without someone to read it; no one would prepare an argument without someone to hear it. And in the final analysis, the audience is the ultimate judge of the worth of an argument. Even if an argument is prepared in accordance with all of the tests of evidence and argument strategies, it may still be unconvincing to an audience. In this case, the effort of the arguer was wasted.

Let's start by defining an audience as that group of people you wish to convince. This can be an audience in the traditional sense of a physically present group of people, or it can be some other group of people. If you are doing a presentation to a group of people to convince them to purchase some product or some service, they are your audience. That physically present group of people are the ones you are trying to convince. If Ronald Reagan is speaking to the Veterans of Foreign Wars about U.S. policy in Central America, this is probably <u>not</u> his audience in the sense we are talking about. Reagan has <u>no</u> need to convince the VFW to support his foreign policy--they already do. He is using that occasion to convince some other audience (perhaps the American people at large) to support him on this issue.

This audience that is not physically present, we will call a conceptual audience. The conceptual audience is imaginary for the speaker. For while the "American people at large" do exist as physical entities, they are also an idea in the mind of the speaker. Just as speakers use real characteristics of the physical audience to decide what arguments are most likely to be convincing, speakers use imagined characteristics of a conceptual audience to guide them in the selection of arguments. Practice speeches, like those delivered in the classroom situations, should be prepared with a conceptual audience in mind.

But, what kind of a conceptual audience? A conceptual audience is not the physically present audience, but our knowledge of (or conceptualization of) an audience. Conceptual audiences can be divided into the particular and universal. Thus, as illustrated in Figure Three, we can speak of three types of audiences:

FIGURE THREE

THREE TYPES OF AUDIENCE

	Particular	Universal
Physical	Type One	
Conceptual	Type Two	Type Three

We have already described the Type One audience in the example of a sales presentation. This is a physical, particular audience. The conceptual, particular audience is your knowledge of this audience. Thus, the Type Two audience is used to guide our preparation of the sales presentation. The universal audience, Type Three, is our conception of all reasonable and competent people and, thus, is never a physical audience.

Public speakers speak to physical (Type One) audiences, but use their conceptual audiences (Types Two and Three) as tools to guide their selection of evidence and argumentation strategies. In this chapter we have frequently talked about a "skeptical audience." This is our Type Three audience. Making an argument strong enough to convince this audience is our task.

Standards of Good Arguments

But what standards do universal audiences use to judge arguments? Perelman and Toulmin convinced us that they do not use formal logic. What is left? Although they do not use the concept of audience in the same manner that we do, Canadian philosophers Ralph H. Johnson and J. Anthony Blair (1983) have defined a "fallacy" in a way that may allow us to tentatively answer this question. They claim that an argument must satisfy standards of relevance, sufficiency, and acceptability and that "any argument which fails to satisfy one (or more) of these requirements is a fallacious argument" (34). What they fail to consider is that an audience is necessary to judge each of these standards, but their idea seems to be a worthwhile starting point.

The Standard of Relevance

This standard means that the evidence and argument must be relevant to the conclusion. If the audience judges the speaker's argument and/or evidence to be irrelevant to the claim, the persuasive attempt is doomed to failure. A commercial for a popular pain reliever says "in studies at a major hospital, XXXXX proved more effective for pain other than headaches. So, the next time you have a headache try XXXXX." The message is trying to convince you to use XXXXX for relief of headaches but the evidence concerned pain other than headaches. Some audiences might never notice this fact. Others would consider the evidence relevant since headaches are similar to other forms of pain. A skeptical audience might question the relevance of the evidence. After all, if XXXXX is so effective for headaches, why was the study limited to pain other than headaches. There must be plenty of people in hospitals with headaches--why weren't these people included in the study. So, speakers need to consider the reaction of a Type Three audience and make their arguments and evidence so clearly relevant that even this skeptical audience will agree.

The Standard of Sufficiency

This standard is imposed when an audience judges that the speaker's argument and evidence, although relevant, are insufficient to be convincing. Imagine that a speaker is trying to convince us that a certain U.S. oil company is sincerely interested in protection of the environment. The evidence the speaker presents consists of a description of an off-shore oil rig that was built with particular attention to the plants and animals living around the rig. Now, this evidence is certainly relevant to the claim, but is it sufficient? A Type Three audience might ask whether this was true of all or most oil rigs that this company installs or whether this one was built as a publicity gimmick? Unless the audience is convinced that this is enough evidence, the argument fails the test of sufficiency.

The Standard of Acceptability

This standard indicates that even evidence that is relevant and sufficient must also be believable. Pretend that, in our previous example, the speaker gave enough examples that we could not deny the standard of sufficiency. A Type Three audience might still not believe the evidence. They might ask the speaker "What is the source of your evidence?", "Can you verify this evidence?" So the best way a speaker can be sure to meet the standard of acceptability is to provide credible and verifiable sources for the evidence.

As the field of argumentation moves away from formal logic toward informal or everyday theories of argumentation, the kinds of advice we have given, in this section, will be improved. At this point, what we are able to say is be careful to select evidence and argument strategies in ways that ensure that audiences will be convinced that your arguments meet the standards of relevance, sufficiency, and acceptability.

DEFENSIVENESS AS A ROADBLOCK TO PERSUASION

So far, we have tried to show how to use yourself and argumentation as sources of persuasion. The paradox is, however, that while effective argumentation is necessary in persuasion, it also causes people to become defensive about their points of view and, thus, becomes a roadblock. In this section, we will discuss the psychological processes that lead to defensiveness and provide some suggestions for overcoming this problem.

How Argumentation Creates Defensiveness

Psychological theories of attitude change promoted by scholars like Leon Festinger (1957) and others have one element in common. Since the human mind strives for consistency, humans attempt to avoid information that is incompatible with their attitudes, values and beliefs. Although these consistency theories have not proven to be an adequate account of the process of persuasion, the central idea that humans strive for consistency seems reasonable.

So, how is this principle of consistency relevant to argumentation and persuasion? Since argumentation deals with issues of controversy, anyone using argumentation as a tool of persuasion must, by necessity, confront another person or an audience with information that is incompatible with their values. If a speaker only told the audience things they already agreed with, persuasion would not be possible. So, the use of argumentation necessitates confrontation of ideas.

How do we react when others confront their attitudes, values and beliefs? We get defensive. In fact, if the attack is serious, most of us get so defensive that before we know what has happened we think the speaker is attacking us--not our ideas. So, we do everything we can to keep from being persuaded.

In fact, the principle of consistency is so strong that people will do many things to avoid being persuaded. We can envision a variety of ways that people employ to deal with confrontation and persuasion as the means of last resort.

First, we do what we can to avoid information that is inconsistent with our attitudes. If we are against abortion, we avoid pro-choice speakers unless our objective is to heckle. Likewise, if we are against capital punishment we don't listen to those who favor the death penalty.

Second, if we cannot avoid this kind of information, we may misperceive it. If we accidentally hear evidence that shows how capital punishment is an effective deterrent, our mind's power of selective perception allows us to misconstrue this evidence to suit our own purposes.

Third, if we cannot avoid and do not misperceive, we may mentally refute the speaker as the speech is being delivered. We have all had this experience. A political candidate that we despise is debating our favorite candidate and while this person is speaking we just sit there and say things like "How silly! I can't believe the stupid things she is saying! How preposterous! Hasn't she even read a newspaper lately."

Fourth, if we do not avoid or misperceive and are unable to refute, we seek information to support our previous beliefs. So, we hear a speech that, while inconsistent with our attitudes and values, was very persuasive. We leave the setting convinced but very uncomfortable with the incompatibilities that the speaker has created for us. So, we talk to our friends or read materials that agree with our original position. And by magic--we return to our original attitudes. Remember our discussion of the "sleeper effect?" Defensiveness seems to be a very good explanation for why the effects of persuasion are short-lived.

Fifth, suppose we have tried all of the four previous alternatives and none of them worked. We then just decide that the issue isn't important enough to worry about. Think of the smoker who has tried all four of our alternatives: tried to avoid information about the health risks, occasionally misperceived information from the surgeon general, tried to refute public service announcements on the television, even tried in vain to find research that refutes the link between smoking and poor health. At this point, the smoker just says "Oh well, it isn't important. I've got to die from something. If smoking doesn't get me something else will!"

The moral of the story is that defensiveness allows us at least these five options _before_ we are persuaded. This should indicate why it is an extremely important topic for anyone seriously interested in the business of persuasion. So, we should devote our attention to some means available for counteracting defensiveness.

Techniques For Avoiding Defensiveness

The truth of the matter is that no perfect means exist for avoiding defensiveness. Some of the techniques we will present are supported by solid evidence. Others are fairly speculative. Defensiveness is such a problem that speakers do not have the luxury of only using techniques that have been thoroughly researched and supported. Speakers need to consider all of the available means and select wisely from them.

Use a Balanced Approach.

Research has demonstrated that a presentation that fairly treats both sides of a question is more effective than a presentation that only represents one viewpoint. This should come as no surprise. If a speaker appears to be fair-minded, even though we may disagree with the ideas being presented, we tend to react by being more open-minded ourselves.

Presenting a balanced message is an approach that we can take with almost any topic. What we need to do is examine our audience's point of view and be sure to show how we understand and appreciate it by presenting arguments favoring both sides of the question. Of course, we still support our position in the end but we do it in a fair and open-minded way.

Present Yourself As a Reluctant Source.

Imagine a former nuclear physicist speaking against nuclear power. "Until yesterday, I had spent twenty-three years working in the nuclear industry. This was my source of income, my livelihood. But, yesterday, I resigned this position because I simply must speak out about the dangers of nuclear power." The speaker has shown how speaking out works to his personal disadvantage. It cost him his job. This kind of strategy is difficult to ignore. Although a wealth of information is not available on this technique, research has shown that sources are more persuasive when they take positions that seem to work to their personal disadvantage source.

Don't blame the audience.

We get most defensive when someone blames us for bad work or for being the cause of problems. Speakers can avoid this by placing the blame either on themselves or some third party. Occasionally, a business person will be in a situation where she needs to address subordinates in order to get them to improve their performance. If she starts by saying, "We have a problem and it's your fault," she has a long way to go before she is going to get maximum cooperation.

Perhaps she can think of some way to take the blame herself. "We have a problem. It's not your fault. In fact, it's mine. But I really need your help to get it solved." If she can't take the blame herself perhaps she can place the blame somewhere else. "We have a problem. It's really not your fault. Those consultants we had in last year really messed things up with their recommendations, but, nevertheless, I really need you to help me fix this mess." In both of these situations the supervisor is likely to get cooperation from her subordinates if she avoids blaming them.

Inoculate the Audience.

When we were children we were inoculated for polio. A doctor injected a dead or weakened polio virus into our body so that it would build up a defense against polio. A similar kind of inoculation can be accomplished in persuasion. We can present the audience with weakened arguments that support the side opposed to our position so that the audience can build up defenses against information they might encounter later. This approach is referred to by William J. McGuire (1962, 1964) as inoculation theory.

Earlier we claimed that people are sometimes persuaded temporarily only to return to their original position after finding support for their previous attitudes and beliefs. In this kind of a situation, inoculation is an excellent strategy.

In practice, inoculation requires three steps. First, persuade the audience using sound evidence and argumentation. Second, forewarn your audience of opposing points of view and evidence. Tell them what kinds of information they are likely to encounter to support these opposing points of view. Finally, refute the opposing evidence and arguments. McGuire and his colleagues found forewarning alone to be superior to traditional persuasion and a combination of forewarning and refutation to be superior to forewarning alone.

Another interesting finding of the inoculation researchers was that inoculation seems to get stronger with the passage of time. As our body's biological defenses continue to get stronger after the polio inoculation, so do our attitudinal defenses. This is particularly relevant when a concern is the "sleeper effect" or the tendency for persuasion to wear off over time. This research seems to suggest that inoculation may be able to overcome the "sleeper effect."

These are just a few suggestions for overcoming defensiveness. Take your audience's point of view, try to find out why they believe the things they believe, and try to show respect for them as intelligent people.

SUMMARY

In this chapter we have discussed speakers and their argumentation as sources of persuasion as well as the problem of defensiveness. A great deal about persuasion is unknown and may never be known. So persuasion remains an art where we must try to find out our audience's beliefs and creatively design persuasive strategies that have a reasonable chance of success.

REFERENCES

Anderson, K. E. and Clevenger, T. Jr. (1963). "A Summary of Experimental Research in Ethos." Speech Monographs, 30 , pp. 59-78.

Aristotle, Rhetoric.

Boulding, K.E. (1956). The Image. Ann Arbor: University of Michigan Press.

Bryant, D. C., & Wallace, K. R. (1969). Fundamentals of Public Speaking (4th ed.). New York: Appleton-Century-Crofts.

Bruskin, R.H. and Associates. London Sunday Times, October 7, 1973.

Dance, F. E. X., & Zak-Dance, C. C. (1986). Public Speaking. New York: Harper & Row.

Ehninger, D. & Brockriede, W. (1963). Decision By Debate. New York: Dodd, Mead & Company.

Festinger, L. A. (1957). A Theory of Cognitive Dissonance. Evanston: Row Peterson.

Foulke, E. and Sticht, T. G., (1966). "The Intelligibility and Comprehension of Time Compressed Speech," Proceedings of the Louisville Conference on Time Compressed Speech, Louisville, Chapters 2 and 3.

Hovland, C. I. and Weiss, W. (1951). "The Influence of Source Credibility on Communication Effectiveness," Public Opinion Quarterly, 15, 635-50.

Izard, C. E. (1977). Human Emotions. New York: Plenum Press.

Johannesen, R. L. (1983). Ethics in Human Communication. Prospect Heights, Ill.: Waveland Press.

Johnson, R. H. and J. A. Blair. (1983). Logical Self-Defense. (2nd ed.) Toronto: McGraw Hill-Ryerson.

Lucas, S. E. (1983). The Art of Public Speaking. New York: Random House.

May, R. (1977). The Meaning of Anxiety. New York: W. W. Norton and Co.

McCroskey, J. C. (1970), "Measures of Communication Bound Anxiety." Speech Monographs, 37, pp. 269-77.

McGuire, W. J. and Papageoris, D. (1961). "The Relative Efficacy of Various Types of Prior Belief-Defense in Producing Immunity Against Persuasion," Journal of Abnormal and Social Psychology, 62, pp. 327-37.

Mehrabian, A. (1972) Nonverbal Communication. Chicago: Aldine-Atherton.

Perelman, Ch. and L. Olbrechts-Tyteca. (1958). La Nouvelle Rhetorique: Traite de l'Argumentation. Paris: Presses Universitaires des France.

Sprague, J., & Stuart, D. (1984). The Speaker's Handbook. New York: Harcourt Brace Jovanovich.

Thrash, A., & Sisco, J. I. (1984). The Basic Skills of Effective Public Speaking. Minneapolis: Burgess Publishing.

Wilson, J. F., & Arnold, C. C. (1974). Public Speaking as Liberal Art (3rd ed.). Boston: Allyn & Bacon.

The Interstate Oratorical Associaton. (1967). Winning Orations of the Interstate Oratorical Association. Mankato, MN: Author.

The Interstate Oratorical Association. (1984). Winning Orations of the Interstate Oratorical Association. Mankato, MN: Author.

The Interstate Oratorical Association. (1985). Winning Orations of the Interstate Oratorical Association. Mankato, MN: Author.

Toulmin, S. (1958). The Uses of Argument. Cambridge: Cambridge University Press.

APPENDIX ONE

<u>Course Policies for Public Speaking</u>

Course Policies for Public Speaking

Course Requirements

Each student is expected to: (1) attend all lectures and laboratory sessions, (2) present a typewritten outline of each speech in advance of its delivery, (3) read all assignments from the textbook by the date assigned, (4) take the final examination, and (5) present four speeches on the dates assigned.

Speeches

(1) The purpose of speech one is diagnostic. The speech will be criticized, but will not be graded. The focus of the criticism will be on speech composition and visual aids (if applicable). Speech one should be three minutes long. This speech is required as a condition of passing the course.

(2) The focus of speech two is to impart some information to the class. Demonstrations and visual aids are especially appropriate in this speech; the use of a visual aid is required. The focus of criticism will be speech composition, visual aids, and delivery. The focus of grading will be speech composition and visual aids. Speech two should be five minutes long.

(3) The focus of speech three involves the presentation of some information to the class followed by a question and answer period. The focus of criticism and grading will be delivery and question and answer. Speech three should be five minutes long; one minute to the speech and four minutes to the question and answer period. The one minute speech should be a simple restatement of ideas from speech one or two.

(4) The focus of speech four involves the presentation of some controversial argument to the class in a manner that respects the principles of persuasion. Since this is your final speech, criticism and grading will focus on all of the skills learned in the class. Due to time pressures in the course, we may be unable to have oral criticism of this speech. Speech four should be six minutes long; four minutes to the speech and two minutes to the question and answer period.

Attendance

Attendance at laboratory sessions is mandatory. This is especially important since this is a public speaking class and the public speaking situation requires an audience. We realize that emergencies occur that may require you to be absent, therefore we will automatically excuse three absences provided they do not occur when you are scheduled to speak. Your grade may be reduced by three percentage points for each absence in excess of these three.

In accordance with our principlesof free speech, members of an audience should refrain from activities which would interfere with the speaker's freedom of speech. Therefore, the lab instructor retains the right to reduce the grade of any student who behaves in ways that disrupt any speaker.

Make-up Speeches

Because of the serious time pressure in this course, you may not be able to make up a speech regardless of the cause of your absence. Only when your absence was a result of a bonafide illness or emergency will you be able to make up a speech. In those cases where your laboratory instructor is able to find class time for you to make up your speech, the grade on that speech will be reduced by one letter. In cases where the absence was the result of an extreme emergency, the reduction of the speech grade is appealable to the course director.

Speech Outlines

Speech one outlines are due the day of the speech. Speech two outlines are due one week prior to the speech. The outlines for this speech will be evaluated by your instructor and returned the next class period so you can revise and resubmit the outline on the day of your speech. Speech three and speech four outlines are due the day of the speech. At the option of the student, these outlines can be given to the instructor for comments one week prior to the speech and resubmitted on the date of the speech.

Time Limits

The time limits for the speeches must be followed closely. Any deviation from the time limits in excess of 30 seconds may result in the grade being lowered.

Constructive Criticism

The instructor will provide individual written criticism of every speech and will provide oral criticism of all speehes at the end of each class period. This criticism will be constructive-- designed to help you improve your speeches.

Grading Scale

One grade will be calculated as a combination of the activities in lecture and laboratory. The final grades will be rounded upward at 89.50, 79.50, 69.50, and 59.60. The final grade will be based on the following percentages:

Speech one	0%
Speech two	20%
Speech three	20%
Speech four	30%
Final examination	30%
TOTAL	100%

Our grading practices are based on what we consider to be high standards for public speaking. The following statements are descriptive of the grading policies that will be followed in this course:

F   indicates that a speech is far enough below the minimum standards that it is considered a failing effort.

D   indicates that a speech is below the minimum standards, yet not so far below that it is considered failing.

C   indicates that a speech meets the minimum standards.

B   indicates that a speech exceeds the minimum standards.

A   indicates that a speech greatly exceeds the minimum standards.

Plagiarism

Plagiarism, the use of another's ideas or words as if they are your own, may result in failure in the class plus other measures that may be taken consistent with university policy.

APPENDIX TWO

<u>Measuring Standards For Public Speaking</u>

Speech Composition Measurement Scales

Level 1: Fails to meet minimal standards.
Level 2: Meets minimal standards.
Level 3: Exceeds minimal standards.

Criteria

1. Introduction
   LEVEL 2: The speaker fulfills the four objectives of the introduction.
   LEVEL 3: The speaker fulfills the four objectives of the introduction in a way that substantially contributes to the overall objectives of the speech.
2. Internal Previews and Summaries
   LEVEL 2: The speaker signposts main points before delivering them and summarizes before proceeding to another point.
   LEVEL 3: The speaker uses signposts and summaries in a way that substantially contributes to the overall effectiveness of the speech.
3. Transitions
   LEVEL 2: The speaker uses clear transitions between main points.
   LEVEL 3: The speaker uses clear transitions between main points in a way that substantially contributes to the overall effectiveness of the speech.
4. Organizational Patterns
   LEVEL 2: The speaker condenses the important ideas in the speech into a small number of main points and organizes them according to a recognizable pattern.
   LEVEL 3: The speaker organizes the speech in such a way that the organizational pattern significantly contributes to the development of the thesis.
5. Support/Explanation
   LEVEL 2: The supporting material is adequate to convince a relatively unbiased person that the arguments are probable, or the explanations are clear enough that a reasonable person could easily follow them.
   LEVEL 3: The supporting material has source citations where appropriate and is so strong that even a person biased in the other direction would be convinced that the speaker had made the best case available, or the explanations are so clear and vivid that a reasonable person can follow them with little or no effort.
6. Conclusion
   LEVEL 2: The speaker fulfills the two objectives of a conclusion.
   LEVEL 3: The speaker fulfills the two objectives of a conclusion in ways that substantially contribute to the overall ovjective of the speech.
7. Topic
   LEVEL 2: The topic is appropriate for a classroom speech.

Standards for Evaluation

Grade of F: Fails to meet two or more criteria at level 2.
Grade of D: Fails to meet one criterion at level 2.
Grade of C: Meets all criteria at level 2.
Grade of B: Meets all criteria at level 2 and four at level 3.
Grade of A: Meets all criteria at level 2 and five at level 3

Visual Aids Measurement Scales

Level 1: Fails to meet minimal standards.
Level 2: Meets minimal standards.
Level 3: Exceeds minimal standards.

Criteria

I. Design and Creation of the Audio-Visual Aid
    LEVEL 2: The design and creation of the aid satisfies minimal standards in the following areas: (a) visibility or audibility, (b) appropriateness to the speech goals, (c) focusing attention on specific material, (d) appropriateness for the audience, and (e) creation according to guidelines in the text.
    LEVEL 3: The design and creation of the aid exceeds minimal standards in the areas mentioned above.

II. Coordination of Audio-Visual and Oral Message
    LEVEL 2: The speaker meets minimal standards for coordination of the aid with the oral message by: (a) simplifying complex ideas or data, (b) creating or enhancing a mood, (c) introducing the aid appropriately, and (d) using appropriate transitions between the aid and the speech.
    LEVEL 3: The speaker exceeds minimal standards for coordination of the aid with the oral message as demonstrated by excellence in the 4 elements listed above.

III. Delivery of the Audio-Visual Portion of the Message
    LEVEL 2: The speaker meets minimal standards for delivery of the audio-visual portion of the message in the following areas: (a) positioning himself/herself appropriately when using the aid, (b) adjusting the sound, image, or positioning of the aid, (c) using equipment effectively, (d) maintaining contact with the audience, and (e) revealing and concealing the aid when appropriate.
    LEVEL 3: The speaker exceeds minimal standards for delivery of the audio-visual portion of the aid with respect to the elements listed above.

IV. Interpretation of the Aid
    LEVEL 2: The speaker meets minimal standards for interpreting the aid by being accurate, concise, and helping the audience to retain the audio-visual message.
    LEVEL 3: The speaker exceeds minimal standards for interpreting the aid with respect to the elements listed above.

Standards for Evaluation

Grade of F: Fails to meet two or more criteria at level 2.
Grade of D: Fails to meet one criterion at level 2.
Grade of C: Meets all criteria at level 2.
Grade of B: Meets all criteria at level 2 and two criteria at level 3.
Grade of A: Meets all criteria at level 2 and three criteria at level 3

Question And Answer Measurement Scales

Level 1: Fails to meet minimal standards.
Level 2: Meets minimal standards.
Level 3: Exceeds minimal standards.

Criteria

1. Initiation of Interchange
    LEVEL 2: With few errors of delivery, the speaker makes a transition to the question and answer session.
    LEVEL 3: Without errors of delivery, the speaker makes a transition to the question and answer session.
2. Active Listening
    LEVEL 2: With few exceptions the speaker listens actively to the question.
    LEVEL 3: Without exception, the speaker listens actively to the question.
3. Clarification of Question
    LEVEL 2: With few exceptions the speaker engages the questioner in an interaction to make sure that they agree about the nature of the question.
    LEVEL 3: Without exception the speaker engages the questioner in an interaction to make sure that they agree about the nature of the question.
4. Repeats
    LEVEL 2: With few exceptions, the speaker repeats the question to the entire audience.
    LEVEL 3: Without exception, the speaker repeats the question to the entire audience.
5. One-line response
    LEVEL 2: With few exceptions, the speaker gives a one-line answer to the question prior to explaining the answer.
    LEVEL 3: Without exception, the speaker gives a one-line answer to the question prior to explaining the answer.
6. Explanation*
    LEVEL 2: With few exceptions, the speaker gives a brief (no more than 15 second) explanation of the one-line response.
    LEVEL 3: Without exception, the speaker gives a brief (no more than 15 second) explanation of the one-line response.
7. Follow-up
    LEVEL 2: With few exceptions, after answering the question, the speaker returns to the questioner to make sure the question was answered.
    LEVEL 3: Without exception, after answering the question, the speaker returns to the questioner to make sure the question was answered.
8. Closure of the Audience Interchange
    LEVEL 2: With few errors in delivery, the speaker closes the session.
    LEVEL 3: Without errors in delivery, the speaker closes the session.

*This criterion can be excused in cases where the explanation is not needed. In cases where it is consistently excused for a speech, the standards for evaluation below will be adjusted accordingly.

Standards for Evaluation

Grade of F: Fails to meet two or more criteria at level 2.
Grade of D: Fails to meet one criterion at level 2.

Grade of C: Meets all criteria at level 2.
Grade of B: Meets all criteria at level 2 and seven criteria at level 3.
Grade of A: Meets all criteria at level 2 and at level 3

Delivery Measurement Scales

<u>Level 1</u>: Fails to meet minimal standards.
<u>Level 2</u>: Meets minimal standards.
<u>Level 3</u>: Exceeds minimal standards.

Criteria

1. UNOBTRUSIVENESS--Delivery that is free of major distractions and does not call attention to itself.
    LEVEL 2: Audible and/or visual elements of delivery are somewhat distracting but not to the point where it is difficult to pay attention to the speaker's message.
    LEVEL 3: Audible and visual elements of delivery do not divert attention from the speaker's message.
2. INTELLIGIBILITY--Delivery that is clear and comprehensible.
    LEVEL 2: Articulation, volume, and rate of speech do not make it difficult to understand the speaker's message.
    LEVEL 3: Articulation, volume, and rate of speech add substantially to the clarity of the speaker's message.
3. FLUENCY--Delivery that is free of unnecessary hesitations.
    LEVEL 2: The number of filled or unfilled pauses do not exceed what might be expected in ordinary conversation.
    LEVEL 3: The speaker's preparation or knowledge is obvious due to the relative absence of filled or unfilled pauses.
4. DYNAMISM--Delivery that expresses an interest in the topic.
    LEVEL 2: Audible and visual elements of delivery suggest that the speaker is interested in the topic.
    LEVEL 3: Audible and visual elements of delivery suggest that the speaker is very interested in the topic.
5. DIRECTNESS--Delivery that expresses an interest in the audience.
    LEVEL 2: An acceptable level of eye contact suggests that the speaker is interested in building rapport with the audience.
    LEVEL 3: Eye contact, movement, and vocal intonation, suggest that the speaker is very interested in building rapport with the audience.

Standards for Evaluation

<u>Grade of F</u>: Fails to meet two or more criteria at level 2.
<u>Grade of D</u>: Fails to meet one criterion at level 2.
<u>Grade of C</u>: Meets all criteria at level 2.
<u>Grade of B</u>: Meets all criteria at level 2 and three criteria at level 3.
<u>Grade of A</u>: Meets all criteria at level 2 <u>and</u> five criteria at level 3

Persuasive Argumentation Measurement Scales

Level 1: Fails to meet minimal standards.
Level 2: Meets minimal standards.
Level 3: Exceeds minimal standards.

Criteria

1. Non-defensive techniques
    Level Two: The speaker utilizes one of the four methods suggested in lecture to avoid defensiveness on the part of the audience.
    Level Three: The speaker's use of one of these methods is so effective that it would probably have caused an audience to attend to a message which might otherwise have caused defensiveness

2. Establishing competence and trustworthiness
    Level Two: The speaker utilizes one or more of the methods suggested in lecture to demonstrate competence and trustworthiness.
    Level Three: The speaker's use of methods suggested in lecture is accomplished in such a manner that the audience perceives him or her to be especially credible on this topic.

3. Standard of Relevance
    Level Two: Evidence and arguments were relevent to the claims from the perspective of most audiences.
    Level Three: Evidence and arguments were relevent to the claims from the perspective of a skeptical audience.

4. Standard of Sufficiency
    Level Two: Evidence and arguments were sufficient to establish the claims according to most audiences.
    Level Three: Evidence and arguments were sufficient to establish the claims according to a skeptical audiences.

5. Standard of Acceptability
    Level Two: Evidence and arguments were sufficiently documented to be acceptable to most audiences.
    Level Three: Evidence and arguments were sufficiently documented to be acceptable to a skeptical audience.

6. Problematicness of Claim
    Level Two: The topic of the speech is sufficiently controversial to constitute a "significant argument."

Standards for Evaluation

Grade of F: Fails to meet two or more criteria at level 2.
Grade of D: Fails to meet one criterion at level 2.
Grade of C: Meets all criteria at level 2.
Grade of B: Meets all criteria at level 2 and four criteria at level 3.
Grade of A: Meets all criteria at level 2 and five criteria at level 3.

APPENDIX THREE

Evaluation Forms For Public Speaking

Grade Computation Chart

Grade Computation: Use the following sheet to compute your grade as the quarter progresses.

Activity	Letter Grade	Raw Score	Percent	Weighted Score
Speech 1			00	
Speech 2			20	
Speech 3			20	
Speech 4			30	
Final Exam			30	
TOTAL			1.00	

COMM 110 COURSE EVALUATION

INSTRUCTIONS: DO NOT PUT YOUR NAME ON THE IBM SHEET. DO NOT WRITE ON THIS FORM. RECORD YOUR RESPONSES ON THE IBM SHEET. PLEASE RATE EACH ITEM ON THE ANSWER SHEET WITH 1 BEING LOW AND 5 BEING HIGH.

EVALUATION OF COURSE AS A WHOLE

1.   Clarity of course objectives.   1 2 3 4 5
2.   Textbook--overall rating.   1 2 3 4 5
3.   Speech One (diagnostic).   1 2 3 4 5
4.   Speech Two (Informative).   1 2 3 4 5
5.   Speech Three (Question & Answer). 1 2 3 4 5
6.   Speech Four (Persuasive).   1 2 3 4 5
7.   Final Examination   1 2 3 4 5
8.   I would recommend this course to others   1 2 3 4 5

LABORATORY EVALUATION

9.   Instructor appears interested in students   1 2 3 4 5
10. Instructor appears to enjoy teaching   1 2 3 4 5
11. Instructor motivates me to do my best work 1 2 3 4 5
12. Quantity of oral criticism   1 2 3 4 5
13. Quality of oral criticism   1 2 3 4 5
14. Quantity of written criticism   1 2 3 4 5
15. Quality of written criticism   1 2 3 4 5
16. Timeliness of written criticism 1 2 3 4 5
17. Instructor's grading practices--overall rating   1 2 3 4 5
18. In comparison to all other college instructors I   1 2 3 4 5
     have had, I would rate this instructor.

LECTURE EVALUATION

19. Instructor is knowledgable in subject matter 1 2 3 4 5
20. Instructor encourages student participation 1 2 3 4 5
     (welcomes questions and discussions).
21. Instructor appears interested in students   1 2 3 4 5
22. Instructor appears to enjoy teaching   1 2 3 4 5
23. Instructor makes material clear to me   1 2 3 4 5
24. Instructor appears prepared and organized in 1 2 3 4 5
     presentations
25. In comparison to all other college instructors   1 2 3 4 5
     I have had, I would rate this instructor.

ADDITIONAL COMMENTS SHOULD BE PLACED ON THE BACK OF YOUR IBM SHEET.

Speech One Evaluation Form

NAME _____

Speech Composition   Speech Composition Grade: _____

1. Introduction   1   2   3
2. Internal Summaries   1   2   3
3. Transitions   1   2   3
4. Organizational Patterns   1   2   3
5. Support/Explanations   1   2   3
6. Conclusion   1   2   3
7. Topic   1   2

Visual Aids   Visual Aids Grade: _____

1. Design and Creations   1   2   3
2. Coordination   1   2   3
3. Delivery   1   2   3
4. Interpretation   1   2   3

GRADE COMPUTATION

Criteria	Letter Grade	Raw Score	Percent	Weighted Score
Outline			10	
Composition			50	
Visual Aids			40	
			TOTAL	_____
			OVERALL GRADE	_____

Speech One Evaluation Form

NAME_____

Speech Composition   Speech Composition Grade:_____

1. Introduction   1   2   3
2. Internal Summaries   1   2   3
3. Transitions   1   2   3
4. Organizational Patterns   1   2   3
5. Support/Explanations   1   2   3
6. Conclusion   1   2   3
7. Topic   1   2

Visual Aids   Visual Aids Grade:_____

1. Design and Creations   1   2   3
2. Coordination   1   2   3
3. Delivery   1   2   3
4. Interpretation   1   2   3

GRADE COMPUTATION

Criteria	Letter Grade	Raw Score	Percent	Weighted Score
Outline			10	
Composition			50	
Visual Aids			40	
		TOTAL		_____
		OVERALL GRADE		_____

Audio-Visual Aid Tabulation
Speech One

Criteria	Audio-Visual Aids				Comments

Design and Creation of Aid	Aid 1	Aid 2	Aid 3	Aid 4
Visible or Audible	1 2 3	1 2 3	1 2 3	1 2 3
Focus Attention	1 2 3	1 2 3	1 2 3	1 2 3
Construction Correct	1 2 3	1 2 3	1 2 3	1 2 3
Appropriate for Topic	1 2 3	1 2 3	1 2 3	1 2 3
Appropriate for Audience	1 2 3	1 2 3	1 2 3	1 2 3
Total				

Coordination of Audio-Visual to Oral Message				
Simplify complex idea	1 2 3	1 2 3	1 2 3	1 2 3
Enhances mood	1 2 3	1 2 3	1 2 3	1 2 3
Introduce Aid	1 2 3	1 2 3	1 2 3	1 2 3
Transition to Speech	1 2 3	1 2 3	1 2 3	1 2 3
Total				

Delivery of the Audio Visual				
Block Audience	1 2 3	1 2 3	1 2 3	1 2 3
Focus Image/Adjust Audio*	1 2 3	1 2 3	1 2 3	1 2 3
Eye contact	1 2 3	1 2 3	1 2 3	1 2 3
Conceal-Reveal-Conceal*	1 2 3	1 2 3	1 2 3	1 2 3
Machine Used Effectively*	1 2 3	1 2 3	1 2 3	1 2 3
Total				

Communicative Aspect				
Interpretation Accurate	1 2 3	1 2 3	1 2 3	1 2 3
Interpretatioan Concise	1 2 3	1 2 3	1 2 3	1 2 3
Enhance Retention	1 2 3	1 2 3	1 2 3	1 2 3
Confident Style	1 2 3	1 2 3	1 2 3	1 2 3
Total				

* exception may be appropriate.
  1 = ineffective use or missing, 2 = meets minimal standard,
  3 = effective and appropriate

Audio-Visual Aid Tabulation
Speech One

<u>Criteria</u>   <u>Audio-Visual Aids</u>   <u>Comments</u>

<u>Design and Creation of Aid</u>	Aid 1	Aid 2	Aid 3	Aid 4
Visible or Audible	1 2 3	1 2 3	1 2 3	1 2 3
Focus Attention	1 2 3	1 2 3	1 2 3	1 2 3
Construction Correct	1 2 3	1 2 3	1 2 3	1 2 3
Appropriate for Topic	1 2 3	1 2 3	1 2 3	1 2 3
Appropriate for Audience	1 2 3	1 2 3	1 2 3	1 2 3
Total	___	___	___	___

<u>Coordination of Audio-Visual to Oral Message</u>				
Simplify complex idea	1 2 3	1 2 3	1 2 3	1 2 3
Enhances mood	1 2 3	1 2 3	1 2 3	1 2 3
Introduce Aid	1 2 3	1 2 3	1 2 3	1 2 3
Transition to Speech	1 2 3	1 2 3	1 2 3	1 2 3
Total	___	___	___	___

<u>Delivery of the Audio Visual</u>				
Block Audience	1 2 3	1 2 3	1 2 3	1 2 3
Focus Image/Adjust Audio*	1 2 3	1 2 3	1 2 3	1 2 3
Eye contact	1 2 3	1 2 3	1 2 3	1 2 3
Conceal-Reveal-Conceal*	1 2 3	1 2 3	1 2 3	1 2 3
Machine Used Effectively*	1 2 3	1 2 3	1 2 3	1 2 3
Total	___	___	___	___

<u>Communicative Aspect</u>				
Interpretation Accurate	1 2 3	1 2 3	1 2 3	1 2 3
Interpretatioan Concise	1 2 3	1 2 3	1 2 3	1 2 3
Enhance Retention	1 2 3	1 2 3	1 2 3	1 2 3
Confident Style	1 2 3	1 2 3	1 2 3	1 2 3
Total	___	___	___	___

* exception may be appropriate.
  1 = ineffective use or missing, 2 = meets minimal standard,
  3 = effective and appropriate

Audio-Visual Aid Tabulation
Speech One

Criteria	Audio-Visual Aids	Comments

Design and Creation of Aid

	Aid 1	Aid 2	Aid 3	Aid 4
Visible or Audible	1 2 3	1 2 3	1 2 3	1 2 3
Focus Attention	1 2 3	1 2 3	1 2 3	1 2 3
Construction Correct	1 2 3	1 2 3	1 2 3	1 2 3
Appropriate for Topic	1 2 3	1 2 3	1 2 3	1 2 3
Appropriate for Audience	1 2 3	1 2 3	1 2 3	1 2 3
Total				

Coordination of Audio-Visual to Oral Message

Simplify complex idea	1 2 3	1 2 3	1 2 3	1 2 3
Enhances mood	1 2 3	1 2 3	1 2 3	1 2 3
Introduce Aid	1 2 3	1 2 3	1 2 3	1 2 3
Transition to Speech	1 2 3	1 2 3	1 2 3	1 2 3
Total				

Delivery of the Audio Visual

Block Audience	1 2 3	1 2 3	1 2 3	1 2 3
Focus Image/Adjust Audio*	1 2 3	1 2 3	1 2 3	1 2 3
Eye Contact	1 2 3	1 2 3	1 2 3	1 2 3
Conceal-Reveal-Conceal*	1 2 3	1 2 3	1 2 3	1 2 3
Machine Used Effectively*	1 2 3	1 2 3	1 2 3	1 2 3
Total				

Communicative Aspect

Interpretation Accurate	1 2 3	1 2 3	1 2 3	1 2 3
Interpretation Concise	1 2 3	1 2 3	1 2 3	1 2 3
Enhance Retention	1 2 3	1 2 3	1 2 3	1 2 3
Confident Style	1 2 3	1 2 3	1 2 3	1 2 3
Total				

* exception may be appropriate.
1 = ineffective use or missing; 2 = meets minimal standard
3 = effective and appropriate

Speech Two Evaluation Form

NAME_____

Speech Composition   Speech Composition Grade:_____

1.   Introduction   1   2   3
2.   Internal Summaries   1   2   3
3.   Transitions   1   2   3
4.   Organizational Patterns   1   2   3
5.   Support/Explanations   1   2   3
6.   Conclusion   1   2   3
7.   Topic   1   2

Visual Aids   Visual Aids Grade:_____

1.   Design and Creation   1   2   3
2.   Coordination   1   2   3
3.   Delivery   1   2   3
4.   Interpretation   1   2   3

Delivery   Delivery Grade:_____

1.   Unobtrusiveness   1   2   3
2.   Intelligibility   1   2   3
3.   Fluency   1   2   3
4.   Dynamism   1   2   3
5.   Directness   1   2   3

GRADE COMPUTATION

Criteria	Letter Grade	Raw Score	Percent	Weighted Score
Outline			10	
Composition			50	
Visual Aids			40	
Delivery			00	

TOTAL   _____

OVERALL GRADE   _____

Speech Two Evaluation Form

NAME_____

Speech Composition   Speech Composition Grade:_____

1.   Introduction   1   2   3
2.   Internal Summaries   1   2   3
3.   Transitions   1   2   3
4.   Organizational Patterns   1   2   3
5.   Support/Explanations   1   2   3
6.   Conclusion   1   2   3
7.   Topic   1   2

Visual Aids   Visual Aids Grade:_____

1.   Design and Creation   1   2   3
2.   Coordination   1   2   3
3.   Delivery   1   2   3
4.   Interpretation   1   2   3

Delivery   Delivery Grade:_____

1.   Unobtrusiveness   1   2   3
2.   Intelligibility   1   2   3
3.   Fluency   1   2   3
4.   Dynamism   1   2   3
5.   Directness   1   2   3

GRADE COMPUTATION

Criteria	Letter Grade	Raw Score	Percent	Weighted Score
Outline			10	
Composition			50	
Visual Aids			40	
Delivery			00	
			TOTAL	
			OVERALL GRADE	

Speech Two Evaluation Form

NAME _____

Speech Composition   Speech Composition Grade: _____

1. Introduction   1   2   3
2. Internal Summaries   1   2   3
3. Transitions   1   2   3
4. Organizational Patterns   1   2   3
5. Support/Explanations   1   2   3
6. Conclusion   1   2   3
7. Topic   1   2   3

Visual Aids   Visual Aids Grade: _____

1. Design and Creation   1   2   3
2. Coordination   1   2   3
3. Delivery   1   2   3
4. Interpretation   1   2   3

Delivery   Delivery Grade: _____

1. Unobstrusiveness   1   2   3
2. Intelligibility   1   2   3
3. Fluency   1   2   3
4. Dynamism   1   2   3
5. Directness   1   2   3

GRADE COMPUTATION

Criteria	Letter Grade	Raw Score	Percent	Weighted Score
Outline			10	
Composition			50	
Visual Aids			40	
Delivery			00	
TOTAL				
OVERALL GRADE				

Audio-Visual Aid Tabulation
Speech Two

Criteria	Audio-Visual Aids				Comments

Design and Creation of Aid	Aid 1	Aid 2	Aid 3	Aid 4
Visible or Audible	1 2 3	1 2 3	1 2 3	1 2 3
Focus Attention	1 2 3	1 2 3	1 2 3	1 2 3
Construction Correct	1 2 3	1 2 3	1 2 3	1 2 3
Appropriate for Topic	1 2 3	1 2 3	1 2 3	1 2 3
Appropriate for Audience	1 2 3	1 2 3	1 2 3	1 2 3
Total	_____	_____	_____	_____

Coordination of Audio-Visual to Oral Message				
Simplify complex idea	1 2 3	1 2 3	1 2 3	1 2 3
Enhances mood	1 2 3	1 2 3	1 2 3	1 2 3
Introduce Aid	1 2 3	1 2 3	1 2 3	1 2 3
Transition to Speech	1 2 3	1 2 3	1 2 3	1 2 3
Total	_____	_____	_____	_____

Delivery of the Audio Visual				
Block Audience	1 2 3	1 2 3	1 2 3	1 2 3
Focus Image/Adjust Audio*	1 2 3	1 2 3	1 2 3	1 2 3
Eye contact	1 2 3	1 2 3	1 2 3	1 2 3
Conceal-Reveal-Conceal*	1 2 3	1 2 3	1 2 3	1 2 3
Machine Used Effectively*	1 2 3	1 2 3	1 2 3	1 2 3
Total	_____	_____	_____	_____

Communicative Aspect				
Interpretation Accurate	1 2 3	1 2 3	1 2 3	1 2 3
Interpretatioan Concise	1 2 3	1 2 3	1 2 3	1 2 3
Enhance Retention	1 2 3	1 2 3	1 2 3	1 2 3
Confident Style	1 2 3	1 2 3	1 2 3	1 2 3
Total	_____	_____	_____	_____

* exception may be appropriate.
  1 = ineffective use or missing, 2 = meets minimal standard,
  3 = effective and appropriate

Audio-Visual Aid Tabulation
Speech Two

Criteria	Audio-Visual Aids				Comments

Design and Creation of Aid

	Aid 1	Aid 2	Aid 3	Aid 4
Visible or Audible	1 2 3	1 2 3	1 2 3	1 2 3
Focus Attention	1 2 3	1 2 3	1 2 3	1 2 3
Construction Correct	1 2 3	1 2 3	1 2 3	1 2 3
Appropriate for Topic	1 2 3	1 2 3	1 2 3	1 2 3
Appropriate for Audience	1 2 3	1 2 3	1 2 3	1 2 3
Total	___	___	___	___

Coordination of Audio-Visual to Oral Message

Simplify complex idea	1 2 3	1 2 3	1 2 3	1 2 3
Enhances mood	1 2 3	1 2 3	1 2 3	1 2 3
Introduce Aid	1 2 3	1 2 3	1 2 3	1 2 3
Transition to Speech	1 2 3	1 2 3	1 2 3	1 2 3
Total	___	___	___	___

Delivery of the Audio Visual

Block Audience	1 2 3	1 2 3	1 2 3	1 2 3
Focus Image/Adjust Audio*	1 2 3	1 2 3	1 2 3	1 2 3
Eye contact	1 2 3	1 2 3	1 2 3	1 2 3
Conceal-Reveal-Conceal*	1 2 3	1 2 3	1 2 3	1 2 3
Machine Used Effectively*	1 2 3	1 2 3	1 2 3	1 2 3
Total	___	___	___	___

Communicative Aspect

Interpretation Accurate	1 2 3	1 2 3	1 2 3	1 2 3
Interpretatioan Concise	1 2 3	1 2 3	1 2 3	1 2 3
Enhance Retention	1 2 3	1 2 3	1 2 3	1 2 3
Confident Style	1 2 3	1 2 3	1 2 3	1 2 3
Total	___	___	___	___

* exception may be appropriate.
  1 = ineffective use or missing, 2 = meets minimal standard,
  3 = effective and appropriate

Audio-Visual Aid Tabulation
Speech Two

Criteria	Audio-Visual Aids				Comments

Design and Creation of Aid

	Aid 1	Aid 2	Aid 3	Aid 4	
Visible or Audible	1 2 3	1 2 3	1 2 3	1 2 3	
Focus Attention	1 2 3	1 2 3	1 2 3	1 2 3	
Construction Correct	1 2 3	1 2 3	1 2 3	1 2 3	
Appropriate for Topic	1 2 3	1 2 3	1 2 3	1 2 3	
Appropriate for Audience	1 2 3	1 2 3	1 2 3	1 2 3	
Total					

Coordination of Audio-Visual to Oral Message

Simplify complex idea	1 2 3	1 2 3	1 2 3	1 2 3	
Enhances mood	1 2 3	1 2 3	1 2 3	1 2 3	
Introduce Aid	1 2 3	1 2 3	1 2 3	1 2 3	
Transition to Speech	1 2 3	1 2 3	1 2 3	1 2 3	
Total					

Delivery of the Audio Visual

Block Audience	1 2 3	1 2 3	1 2 3	1 2 3	
Focus Image/Adjust Audio*	1 2 3	1 2 3	1 2 3	1 2 3	
Eye Contact	1 2 3	1 2 3	1 2 3	1 2 3	
Conceal-Reveal-Conceal*	1 2 3	1 2 3	1 2 3	1 2 3	
Machine Used Effectively*	1 2 3	1 2 3	1 2 3	1 2 3	
Total					

Communicative Aspect

Interpretation Accurate	1 2 3	1 2 3	1 2 3	1 2 3	
Interpretation Concise	1 2 3	1 2 3	1 2 3	1 2 3	
Enhance Retention	1 2 3	1 2 3	1 2 3	1 2 3	
Confident Style	1 2 3	1 2 3	1 2 3	1 2 3	
Total					

* exception may be appropriate.

1 = ineffective use or missing, 2 = meets minimal standard
3 = effective and appropriate

Speech Three Evaluation Form

NAME_____

Delivery   Delivery Grade:_____

1.   Unobtrusiveness   1   2   3
2.   Intelligibility   1   2   3
3.   Fluency   1   2   3
4.   Dynamism   1   2   3
5.   Directness   1   2   3

Question and Answer   Question and Answer Grade:_____

1.   Initiation   1   2   3
2.   Active Listening   1   2   3
3.   Clarify the Question   1   2   3
4.   Repeats   1   2   3
5.   One-Line Response   1   2   3
6.   Explanation   1   2   3
7.   Follow-up   1   2   3
8.   Closure   1   2   3

GRADE COMPUTATION

Criteria	Letter Grade	Raw Score	Percent	Weighted Score
Outline			10	
Delivery			45	
Question and Answer			45	

TOTAL   _____

OVERALL GRADE   _____

Speech Three Evaluation Form

NAME_____

<u>Delivery</u>   Delivery Grade:_____

1.	Unobtrusiveness	1	2	3
2.	Intelligibility	1	2	3
3.	Fluency	1	2	3
4.	Dynamism	1	2	3
5.	Directness	1	2	3

<u>Question and Answer</u>   Question and Answer Grade:_____

1.	Initiation	1	2	3
2.	Active Listening	1	2	3
3.	Clarify the Question	1	2	3
4.	Repeats	1	2	3
5.	One-Line Response	1	2	3
6.	Explanation	1	2	3
7.	Follow-up	1	2	3
8.	Closure	1	2	3

GRADE COMPUTATION

Criteria	Letter Grade	Raw Score	Percent	Weighted Score
Outline			10	
Delivery			45	
Question and Answer			45	
			TOTAL	_____
			OVERALL GRADE	_____

Question and Answer Session Tabulation
Speech Three

Criteria

Initiation of Interchange: Comments

    Transition to interchange   1 2 3
      (i.e. ground rules)
    Appropriate Nonverbals   1 2 3
      (i.e. pause, physical movement)

Six Step Model   Question Number

	1	2	3	4	5	6	7
Active Listening							
Negotiate Meaning*							
Restate the Question							
One-line Response							
Explanation*							
Follow-up							

Closure of Interchange   Comments

    Closure statement   1 2 3
    Transition to conclusion   1 2 3
    Nonverbals effective   1 2 3

Closure of Presentation   Comments

    Delivery effective   1 2 3
    Composition effective   1 2 3

* exception may be appropriate. 1 = missing or ineffective use,
  2 = appropriate use, 3 = effective use.

Question and Answer Session Tabulation
Speech Three

Criteria

Initiation of Interchange: Comments

    Transition to interchange   1 2 3
      (i.e. ground rules)
    Appropriate Nonverbals   1 2 3
      (i.e. pause, physical movement)

Six Step Model

Question Number	1	2	3	4	5	6	7
Active Listening							
Negotiate Meaning*							
Restate the Question							
One-line Response							
Explanation*							
Follow-up							

Closure of Interchange   Comments

    Closure statement   1 2 3
    Transition to conclusion   1 2 3
    Nonverbals effective   1 2 3

Closure of Presentation   Comments

    Delivery effective   1 2 3
    Composition effective   1 2 3

* exception may be appropriate. 1 = missing or ineffective use,
  2 = appropriate use, 3 = effective use.

Speech Four Evaluation Form

NAME_____

Speech Composition   Speech Composition Grade:_____
1.   Introduction   1   2   3
2.   Internal Summaries   1   2   3
3.   Transitions   1   2   3
4.   Organizational Patterns   1   2   3
5.   Support/Explanations   1   2   3
6.   Conclusion   1   2   3
7.   Topic   1   2
Delivery   Delivery Grade:_____
1.   Unobtrusiveness   1   2   3
2.   Intelligibility   1   2   3
3.   Fluency   1   2   3
4.   Dynamism   1   2   3
5.   Directness   1   2   3
Question and Answer   Question and Answer Grade:_____
1.   Initiation   1   2   3
2.   Active Listening   1   2   3
3.   Clarify the Question   1   2   3
4.   Repeats   1   2   3
5.   One-Line Response   1   2   3
6.   Explanation   1   2   3
7.   Follow-up   1   2   3
8.   Closure   1   2   3
Persuasive Argumentation   Persuasion Grade:_____
1.   Non-defensive techniques   1   2   3
2.   Establishing credibility   1   2   3
3.   Standard of Relevance   1   2   3
4.   Standard of Sufficiency   1   2   3
5.   Standard of Acceptability   1   2   3
6.   Problematicness of Claim   1   2   3

GRADE COMPUTATION

Criteria	Letter Grade	Raw Score	Percent	Weighted Score
Outline			10	
Composition			20	
Delivery			20	
Question and answer			15	
Persuasion			35	
		TOTAL		_____
		OVERALL GRADE		_____

STUDENT COPY   181

Speech Four Evaluation Form

NAME_____

Speech Composition				Speech Composition Grade:_____

Speech Composition   Speech Composition Grade:_____
1. Introduction   1   2   3
2. Internal Summaries   1   2   3
3. Transitions   1   2   3
4. Organizational Patterns 1   2   3
5. Support/Explanations   1   2   3
6. Conclusion   1   2   3
7. Topic   1   2

Delivery   Delivery Grade:_____
1. Unobtrusiveness   1   2   3
2. Intelligibility   1   2   3
3. Fluency   1   2   3
4. Dynamism   1   2   3
5. Directness   1   2   3

Question and Answer   Question and Answer Grade:_____
1. Initiation   1   2   3
2. Active Listening   1   2   3
3. Clarify the Question   1   2   3
4. Repeats   1   2   3
5. One-Line Response   1   2   3
6. Explanation   1   2   3
7. Follow-up   1   2   3
8. Closure   1   2   3

Persuasive Argumentation   Persuasion Grade:_____
1. Non-defensive techniques 1   2   3
2. Establishing credibility 1   2   3
3. Standard of Relevance   1   2   3
4. Standard of Sufficiency 1   2   3
5. Standard of Acceptability 1   2   3
6. Problematicness of Claim 1   2   3

GRADE COMPUTATION

Criteria	Letter Grade	Raw Score	Percent	Weighted Score
Outline			10	
Composition			20	
Delivery			20	
Question and answer			15	
Persuasion			35	
		TOTAL		_____
		OVERALL GRADE		_____

Speech Code Evaluation Form

NAME _____

| Speech Composition | | Speech Composition Grade _____ |
| 1. Introduction |
| 2. Internal Summaries |
| 3. Transitions |
| 4. Organizational Patterns |
| 5. Support/Explanations |
| 6. Conclusion |
| 7. Topic |

| Delivery | | Delivery Grade _____ |
| 1. Unobtrusiveness |
| 2. Intelligibility |
| 3. Fluency |
| 4. Dynamism |
| 5. Directness |

| Question and Answer | | Question and Answer Grade _____ |
| 1. Initiation |
| 2. Active Listening |
| 3. Clarify the Question |
| 4. Repeats |
| 5. One-Line Response |
| 6. Explanation |
| 7. Follow-up |
| 8. Closure |

| Persuasive Argumentation | | Persuasion Grade _____ |
| 1. Non-defensive techniques |
| 2. Establishing credibility |
| 3. Standard of Relevance |
| 4. Standard of Sufficiency |
| 5. Standard of Acceptability |
| 6. Problematicness of Claim |

GRADE COMPUTATION

Criteria	Letter Grade	Raw Score	Percent	Weighted Score
Outline			10	
Composition			40	
Delivery			20	
Question and answer			15	
Persuasion			15	
TOTAL				

OVERALL GRADE _____

Question and Answer Session Tabulation
Speech Four

Criteria

<u>Initiation of Interchange:</u>   <u>Comments</u>

    Transition to interchange   1 2 3
      (i.e. ground rules)
    Appropriate Nonverbals   1 2 3
      (i.e. pause, physical movement)

<u>Six Step Model</u>   Question Number

	1	2	3	4	5	6	7
Active Listening							
Negotiate Meaning							
Restate the Question							
One-line Response							
Explanation*							
Follow-up							

<u>Closure of Interchange</u>   <u>Comments</u>

    Closure statement   1 2 3
    Transition to conclusion 1 2 3
    Nonverbals effective   1 2 3

<u>Closure of Presentation</u>   <u>Comments</u>

    Delivery effective   1 2 3
    Composition effective   1 2 3

* exception may be appropriate. 1 = missing or ineffective use,
  2 = appropriate use, 3 = effective use.

Question and Answer Session Tabulation
Speech Four

Criteria

Initiation of Interchange: Comments

Transition to interchange   1 2 3
(i.e. ground rules)
Appropriate Nonverbals   1 2 3
(i.e. pause, physical movement)

Six Step Model   Question Number

	1	2	3	4	5	6	7
Active Listening							
Negotiate Meaning							
Restate the Question							
One-line Response							
Explanation*							
Follow-up							

Closure of Interchange   Comments

Closure statement   1 2 3
Transition to conclusion   1 2 3
Nonverbals effective   1 2 3

Closure of Presentation   Comments

Delivery effective   1 2 3
Composition effective   1 2 3

* exception may be appropriate. 1 = missing or ineffective use,
  2 = appropriate use, 3 = effective use.

Question and Answer Session Outline for
Speech Four

Criteria

Initiation of Interchange   Comments

  Transition to Interchange
    (i.e. ground rules)
  Appropriate Nonverbals
    (i.e. pause, physical movement)

Six-Step Model   Question Number

                              1   2   3   4

  Active Listening

  Paraphrase Meaning

  Restate the Question

  One-Time Response

  Explanation

  Follow-up

Closure of Interchange   Comments

  Return statement
  Transition to Conclusion
  Nonverbals effective*

Manner of Presentation   Comments

  Verbally effective
  Composition effective

* exception may be appropriate, if missing or ineffective use.
? = appropriate use; ? = effective use